Praise for the *Professional Mom's Guide to Success & Sanity*

"The *Professional Mom's Guide to Success & Sanity* is a thoughtful and useful step-by-step guide for reducing stress and putting you in position to take the actions you want to take. Sheila's writing is both easy to understand and very useful. Is clear how much she cares about her readers."

— Gene Monterastelli, EFT Practitioner & host of the Tapping Q&A Podcast

"Sheila Henry has written a book full of heart-felt stories, powerful exercises, and a strong message: that professional women CAN be powerful, successful, and great moms. She doesn't sugar-coat the fact that it's work, but gives a step-by-step approach to support women on their journey. Professional moms who do this work will find it well worth it!"

— Pamela Bruner, author of *Tapping into Ultimate Success*.

"Here is a powerhouse book of tips, tactics and approaches for stress and overwhelm that simply work. A fantastic book."

— Dale Teplitz, Tapping Guru and EFT Universe Trainer.

PROFESSIONAL MOM'S GUIDE TO SUCCESS AND SANITY

How to Balance Career and Home Life with Less Stress

Sheila Henry, LMFT

PROFESSIONAL MOM'S GUIDE TO SUCCESS AND SANITY
How to Balance Career & Home Life with Less Stress!

ISBN: 978-0-9989447-0-8

Library of Congress Number: 2017908230

Cover Design by Nathaniel Dasco

Dedication

I dedicate this book to my parents, Abe and Rose Garfinkel, who gave me the greatest love that parents could give.

I also dedicate this book to my son, Gregory Mark Henry, who taught me a lot about the importance of being a good parent.

Table of Contents

Introduction

Students in my high school are up in arms. They are throwing tomatoes, shouting words such as, "You, filthy traitor!" The stench of the rotten tomatoes almost overpowers me. I have never seen something like this at our school. I watch in horror as my beloved teacher, Miss Patterson, a fair and caring teacher, is being attacked. She just stands near the door to her room with a bewildered look. I'm too frightened to go near her and stick up for her. I slink past her classroom door, hoping she doesn't see me.

This shy, caring woman gathered all her personal belongings, and the next thing I knew, she left without saying goodbye, never to be spoken about or heard from again.

It really started the night before. I stood staring at the daily newspaper, astonished at what I was seeing. "Local Communists Exposed." My heart and mind were filled with terror. There was a long list of names that included Miss Patterson. The names of my parents were not in that list. But I knew that my parents were involved. Miss Patterson had been an honored guest in my home when my parents hosted meetings of the Communist group in Pittsburgh.

During the McCarthy period, my parents belonged to the Communist Party. Every so often, these basically shy people, with a strong belief in equality of sharing that was the basis of Marxist philosophy, met at my house. (This is not what Stalin was doing at the time in the Soviet Union. But they, like most Communists in the country, didn't know it. Most of the Communists in the country left the Party when they found out what was happening in the Soviet Union.)

I was scared that the paper would publish my parents' names and then the students would throw rotten tomatoes and call me a filthy spy. I was too terrified to even realize that those beliefs were not my beliefs and I was not my parents. For weeks, whenever the newspaper was delivered, I rushed to read the headlines. Although it never happened, I was in a state of terror.

I made a life changing decision. **"It is not safe to let people know who I really am."**

But this unconscious decision of a teenage girl wasn't only for people knowing about my parents' political beliefs, but it spread out and affected my whole life. I didn't really share my inner thoughts or feelings with my friends. When I dated, I didn't let people know who I was. When I started being a counselor, I didn't share with others how I worked or why. This limiting belief, that the world was not a safe place, held me back from the emotional intimacy that I could have had with friends and dates. This didn't serve me, my friends, or my career. It affected my life for decades and I unconsciously treated so many people as unsafe for me. But I did this unconsciously.

We all make decisions and come to certain beliefs—usually by the time we are seven years old. Many of these decisions are mostly unconscious. Some of these decisions are good ones that enable us to lead an empowering life. Others are decisions that hold us back because they interpret the world in ways that harm us. These decisions of an extremely young child are the best ones we can make at the time with the knowledge that we have. We continue believing them without realizing how untrue they are and how they limit us in getting what we want. As adults, we can bring these decisions into our conscious mind and then make a choice about continuing to believe them. We can choose whether these beliefs are ones we want our children to adopt.

Looking at the students shouting at that teacher was very traumatic for me. The belief that I came away with—"It is not safe to let people know who I am"—did not serve me.

After I graduated from college, I moved to California—a long way from Pittsburgh, Pennsylvania. I thought that that part of my life was over. I was starting a new leaf where no one knew me.

But I found myself still following that old limiting belief, **"It is not safe for people to know who I really am."** Obviously that interfered, in a very negative way, with leading a fulfilling life. Unfortunately, we take the decisions we made as a child and let them **unconsciously control our adult life**.

Because of the devastating pain that I felt, my life was limited in many ways. It was many decades later that I came to realize that I had these limiting beliefs holding me back. As I identified, and then changed, the limiting beliefs into empowering ones, my life was transformed. The stress in my life was dramatically reduced.

Most of the time, we do not realize we have limiting beliefs. Instead we experience an inability to reach our goals after much trial and error. We experience a lot of stress from overwhelm, inability to handle the multiple challenges that working mothers face. We can't figure out why this happens. We are plagued with oodles of guilt. Sometimes we call it self-sabotage. Sometimes we're just frustrated. All of this brings a lot of unnecessary stress and suffering in our life. This book will help clear the cobwebs from your mind.

I am writing this book so that you do not have to go through all the suffering that my limitations and stress imposed upon me. I am writing about how to identify these limiting beliefs and change them into empowering ones, thereby lowering stress so that your life can be transformed. As you lower your stress level and accomplish more of your goals, you will realize that you are also helping your children. Children do learn by example and not by the words that we preach to them.

I realized that as we identify and transform all the limiting beliefs that we have, we can have a much more fulfilling life. In my counseling/coaching career I have been able to help many people end years of suffering and frustration. They change their limiting beliefs into enabling beliefs that bring joy into their lives. Just as it enabled me to transform my fear of not being safe, it is my wish that this book will enable you to transform your life. This book contains a distillation of the tools that I use to help professional moms and other people how to combat stress and lead a life they love.

I have included the most powerful cutting edge, scientifically proven tools for you to transform those beliefs. Most of these tools are from EFT (Emotional Freedom Techniques), often known as tapping. A few are from the field of NLP (Neurolinguistic Programming).

There are books on tapping, books on child rearing, and books on stress reduction. I have combined tapping with transforming the core roots of stress. I have also said a few words about child rearing, although this is not a book on child rearing. However, a calm, peaceful, successful mother is a powerful role model for a child. As a parent handles stress, she is also teaching her child to be resilient.

I want to help you realize the hidden cost of stress to your career and family. I also want to pave the way for you to see light at the end of the tunnel. My hope is you will experience a profound transformation as I made and enjoy your life more fully.

How to Read This Book

Why is it that some people succeed in achieving their dream life while others are struggle and accomplish very little? When they are at their best, and life finally starts to work out, they do something that seems stupid to them. They may not know why they do it, but they find themselves repeating the same mistakes over and over, or something happens to stop them in their tracks. The same problems keep recurring. Is it bad luck? Is the world just against them?

As a licensed counselor, I have wondered about this. Is there a way I could effectively help the clients I dealt with achieve their goals? I wasn't satisfied with just making them feel better. I wanted to get to the bottom of what was stopping them so that I could help them heal and eliminate those obstacles. I wanted them to accomplish what they wanted and to feel good about themselves.

Raising children while concurrently having a job is extremely stressful. A lot of the stress is due to the way that we grew up, the way that we view the world, our belief structure, and our habits. Our environment is not set up to ease the burden of combining child care with a career. This affects our children and our career as shown in these examples.

1. Many mothers have not ironed out all the challenges that have come from their upbringing. After a honeymoon period with a mate, they find that oftentimes they have married someone just like one of their parents. Struggles that they have had with their parents in many ways are duplicated in the relationship with their mate. Gerry said that she never wanted her parents to tell her what to do when she was a teenager. Now in her relationship with John she feels that John wants to "lay down the law" about how she should act. Fights ensue.

2. Although they want their children to be more successful than they were, parents find that children oftentimes pick up their habits,

fears and thoughts. This makes it important for parents to handle their childhood issues. When I talk about limiting beliefs, these beliefs limit the way that they and their children can have a fulfilling life. As one mother said, "I need to have control of everything." She was in many fights with one of her children.

3. Although she was a very good businesswoman and negotiator at work, Mildred realized that after a tense discussion, she would go home and mindlessly eat while preparing dinner for her family. She continued to snack after the children were in bed. She had to learn to recognize her stress and handle it in other ways. She lost 25 pounds over a year.

These and other examples spread throughout the book are ones that I have worked with in my practice. Much of the stress we experience in our day-to-day life is rooted in our past. **As parents handle their own stress related problems, the jobs of parenting and work become easier and are handled better.** Mothers hand down their new skills to their children and find childrearing much more pleasant and easier. The jobs at work flow more smoothly. That is why so much of this book is about lowering the stress level.

Read Chapter 1 -- 12 in order. Be sure to do the exercises. Choose which exercises in Chapters 13 – 28 may apply to you. Skip other exercises or change the wording to suit yourself. The wording of the tapping exercises gives you suggestions and helps you learn how to use your own words. I have included many more problems than any one person has. That is so that many different people can learn to handle their individual challenge through reading this book.

This book requires you to do the exercises if you wish to get the benefit of lowering your stress level. In this book, you'll learn how to do EFT or tapping. You will also learn how, by relieving your stress, you will become a better mother and will be giving the finest gift possible to your children. As you are a happy productive parent, your children benefit from the role model that you provide.

A Special Bonus from Sheila

Now that you have your copy of ***Professional Mom's Guide to Success & Sanity,*** you are on your way from being the haggard, frazzled, stressed out mother to the calm, peaceful, and successful woman you were always meant to be. You'll get loads of information and habits to start incorporating into your life.

You'll also receive the special bonus I created to make it easier to do the tapping exercises that are an integral part of this book. I have recorded six "tap along" MP3s to help you become an expert tapper. When you finish this book, you will be armed with the skills to effectively handle many of the challenges that you face as a working mother.

There's so much confusing information out there about stress. Although many techniques work to help you gain calmness momentarily, energy psychology tools (EFT, or "tapping," being one of them) can help that become permanent by removing the core cause of the stress.

Go to http://www.sheilahenry.com/Bonus.en.html to register for your bonus. As another bonus you will also receive tips and information about managing stress from time to time.

The sooner you know how to manage stress, the sooner you'll feel in control.

PART I

UNTANGLE THE THREADS TO CREATE YOUR LIFE GOALS

Chapter 1

Share My Liberating Path (Learning to Take Action)

As parents handle their own stress related problems, the jobs of parenting and work become easier and are handled better.

I had gone to marriage counseling and the therapist asked me, "Why the hell are you still with Bill?" I was startled and thought about the answer for a long time. I had no answer. When my son, Greg, was two years old, I filed for divorce. Luckily for me, I was a teacher in San Francisco and I could support my son and myself. Bill couldn't keep a job and was certainly not a candidate to help with child support. I never looked back upon that decision with any regret.

I was just sure that I would meet another man and that we would get married and start another family. Or perhaps my dream man might also have custody of one or two children and we would have a mixed family.

I continued with counseling and eventually decided that I wanted to become a counselor. I began to think that counseling was the most exciting field in the world and I wanted to be a part of it. I asked my therapist if he would train me. "Sure, just as soon as you get a Master's Degree in Psychology or Social Work." Okay, that seemed like a reasonable request.

I took some prerequisite classes in psychology and began to apply to graduate schools in the area. I had to stay in the area because I had a job that paid money. But I had a problem. To become a teacher in California, I went to UC Berkeley. I had a good GPA as an undergraduate in political science. But I thought that the education courses at Berkeley were the most ridiculous courses I had ever taken. I hated the English courses that I had to take to get a minor. When I finally got my teaching credential, my GPA had too many C grades. This doesn't look good on a graduate program application. So I was turned down by many area colleges.

But I had a **strong intention** to become a counselor. This is why I'm relating this incident to you. A **strong intention** is one of the first elements that you need if you are going to transform your life.

I saw a flier in a grocery store that advertised the two leading marriage therapists of Marin County were going to be giving a course in Marriage Counseling for two weeks. I signed up with the intention of hanging up my shingle after these two weeks. I took the course and in the second week one of the students announced that Sonoma State was opening the Humanistic Psychology Institute (HPI) and was enrolling all applicants with a bachelor's degree. Of course, I enrolled.

I wasn't sure how I would work out the timing. I just enrolled. About a week before the high school where I taught was starting again in September, the principal called a meeting of all the teachers. Because of earthquake standard laws, Galileo High School was going on double session for two years. Each building (there were two) would take a year to renovate. That meant that I would be working half time for full pay for two years.

Several miracles had happened in my life. First, I got enrolled in a school where I could get my master's degree. Second, I could work part time for full pay. I could also do my first internship since I had the time.

The third miracle happened at the end of my first year at HPI. Although the degree that I would get at HPI was a good degree, because of certain regulations at the state level, I would not be eligible to become licensed. A meeting was called between the teachers and interested students of HPI and deans of Lone Mountain College, which was part of the University of San Francisco. They had the desired accreditation so that their graduates would qualify to be licensed. They just didn't have any students and we needed to persuade them to accept students.

About twenty-five students came to that meeting. We all told the deans that they should reopen their school. After a lot of discussion, the dean said he would reopen and accept two or three students. We looked at him with dismay. One man got up and said, "That's unacceptable. You need to accept all or none of us."

The dean was shocked into silence. He blustered out, "I'll accept all students who qualified based on their undergraduate degree." I, along with about twenty other students, transferred over to a great university where our degree would allow us to eventually get a license.

I share this story because I believe that once anyone has a very strong intention about achieving a goal, and they start to take action, then doors will open up.

What gets in the way of so many people that don't achieve their goals? Many people aren't sure of what they want. They are sure about what they don't want or don't like.

For example, a woman might say, "I don't like what my husband does when he comes home. He gets a couple of bottles of beer, puts on the television to some football game, and flops down on the sofa." I'll ask, "What would you like him to do?" She says, "I don't know. Maybe he could just help out." Here she often isn't specific on what he could do to help her out. Or maybe what she really wants is some affection and praise on his part. But she doesn't say it because she believes he should know what to do, and telling him would mean that he doesn't mean it.

Be clear about what you want with another person, a task, or with a career and you have started on the road to success.

Chapter 2

Meet and Conquer Your Inner Critical Voice

Why is the **Inner Critical Voice** so important for mothers? Many of the ideas that children hold on to have come from their parents. Sally wanted $2 to buy a toy. She asked her mother for the money, and her mother replied, "Do you think money grows on trees?" Sally heard that phrase repeated many times. As time passed, she no longer asked her mother for money. She now had ingested the belief that money was scarce. Now she didn't feel like she could have a lot of money. This prevented her from asking her boss for a raise. Then she told her daughter, Emily, that she shouldn't waste money. Sally couldn't ask for more money or expect a lot of money because of her belief that money wasn't easily available. She was teaching this to her daughter. These beliefs can go on for generations. In working with me on her money beliefs, Sally then influenced Emily's beliefs so that her daughter learned that she could get a high paying job. Sally is a now better influence on Emily.

Instead of giving children what they want, or telling them why they can't have it, other parents may say, "Who do you think you are for wanting that? You don't deserve to have that." They grew up believing, "I don't deserve to have what I want." Or, "I'm not good enough to have that."

Perhaps you have noticed that what stops us from achieving what we want is our mindset or that **inner critical voice** inside of us that keeps putting us down, stopping us from believing that we really can have what we want. The exercises in this book show you how to identify this **inner critical voice**, and then how to change it.

We know and we don't know what this voice is saying. If it is holding you back from your desires, you are also training your child to believe it.

Remember, as parents handle their own stress related problems, the jobs of parenting and work become easier and are handled better.

Chapter 3

Choose the Right Path to Create Your Goals

Let's say that you are very clear about what you want. You want to make $X amount of money this next year. You start out by doing your visualizations. But the process of visualizing is not that easy.

When you make affirmations about your goals, you need to visualize yourself taking the action to achieve these goals. It has been shown that when people only visualize themselves having achieved the goal, it often **demotivates** them to take the necessary action because they feel like they have already accomplished their goal.

EXERCISE:

Think about the problems you may have working on the goal.

Visualize yourself working on and conquering the obstacles.

Visualize yourself having achieved these goals.

EXERCISE:

To start with answer the following questions that can help you gain clarity about your vision.

1. What don't you want?
2. What do you want?
3. Why do you want it?
4. What will it do for you if you get it?
5. How will you know when you have it?
6. When, where, and with whom do you want it?
7. How will it affect the other people in your life?
8. How will it affect other things such as my job, finances, and home?

9. What is stopping you from having this already?

10. What resources do you have that will help you obtain it?

11. What additional resources do you need?

12. What are the first steps you are going to take now

Question 9 is extremely important. Spend some time thinking about this.

But then that Inner Critical Voice takes over. It can sound something like:

"I don't deserve to have this."

"I'm not worthy of this."

"This goal is OK for other people to achieve, but not OK for me."

"It's impossible to do this."

There are many discouraging words that that **Inner Critical Voice** might whisper or shout into your ears. That **Inner Critical Voice** needs to be transformed into something helpful. (We'll delve into this important topic in Chapters 12 and 17.)

EXERCISE: Timelines (This is a very powerful exercise!)

1. Mark sheets of paper with the following statements

Now

1 month from now

1 year in future

3 years in future

5 years in future

10 years in future

20 years in the future

1 month ago

1 year ago

3 years ago

5 years ago

10 years ago

20 years ago

2. With your eyes closed, imagine yourself brushing your teeth today. Imagine yourself brushing your teeth a month ago, a year ago, three years ago, five years ago, ten years ago, and twenty years ago. For each of these points you will have a timeline of how you see this in your mind's eye. You are imagining the time (not the brushing). The line you imagine will probably look like one of the illustrations be*low*.

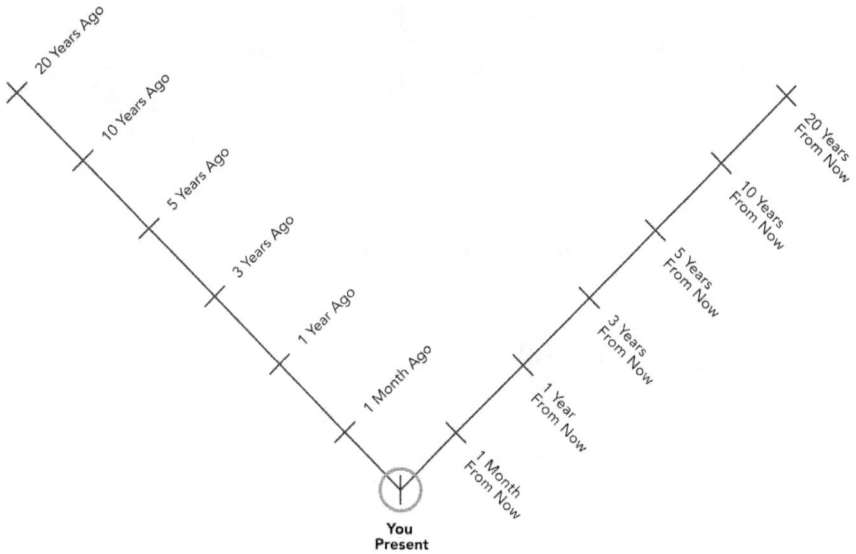

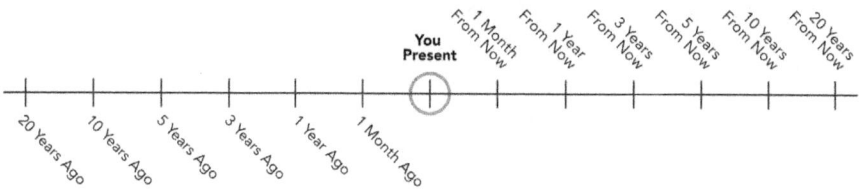

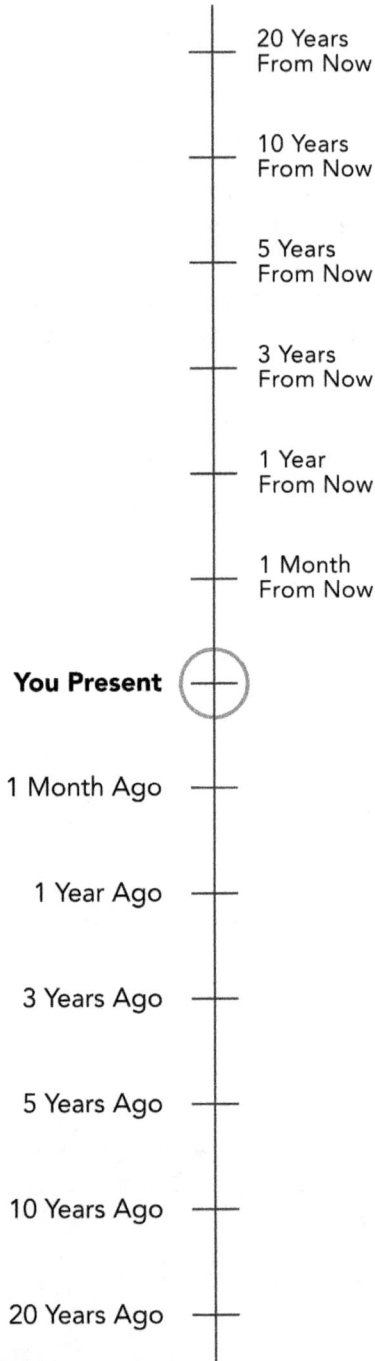

20 Years
From Now

10 Years
From Now

5 Years
From Now

3 Years
From Now

1 Year
From Now

1 Month
From Now

You Present

1 Month Ago

1 Year Ago

3 Years Ago

5 Years Ago

10 Years Ago

20 Years Ago

3. Do the same thing for the future. You imagine drawing the lines where you brush your teeth.

4. Stand in the now position and put the sheets of paper on the floor in the placement as you have imagined it. Look at the past line and see if you have any thoughts about it. Are you learning anything about it as you are looking? How easy is it to see your strengths and weaknesses?

5. Walk on the past timeline. At each point, talk about what important things were happening.

6. When you come to a painful event, step to an earlier time. Ask yourself what you would need to help you get past this point without the pain. Perhaps you might need an older, wiser person that could be the you of today. Perhaps it might be another loving person. Ask them to help you go through this period. Then go to this point in time again with the help of this guide. Feel relieved and as you continue on this journey to the present, imagine your past life and how different it would be if you didn't have this pain. What is your life like when these pains didn't exist?

7. Go back to the present position. Now move forward step by step towards the future. What do you want it to look like? Put your dreams and goals here. Step on top of the papers. As you imagine achieving these goals, how do you feel? Is this what you really want? Are you aiming high enough with your goals?

It is possible to heal some of the past painful points in your life by imagining them to be different. It is also possible to believe more in your positive future if you walk this timeline.

What the Timelines Mean

The timelines that you draw have implications in your life on a day to day basis, as well as decades into the future. If you have a vertical timeline, your past is behind you and it is difficult for you to learn from the past. If your line is horizontal, you are mainly in the present. If you have the V shape, it is easier to learn from the past while also visualizing the future.

Some people enjoy experimenting with different timelines. You might try visualizing time in a different way. Each way has advantages and disadvantages. Try experimenting by utilizing the different time lines.

Some people have the papers all over the place and not in a single line. I worked once with a woman who had that happen. When she played around with timelines, she chose a V shape and later told me that she became more focused in her life. If you have papers all over the place, I strongly suggest you manipulate the papers to one of the three shapes.

Experiment with the different shapes. Play with these shapes. You can always return to your original shape. If this is too hard, you can find a coach who will help guide you through the timeline exercise.

Chapter 4

Take That First Step (The Starting Line)

The next big stumbling block is that a lot of people don't take **action**. As you recall, I made the decision to become a counselor and then took several steps. I took pre-existing psychology courses; I unsuccessfully applied to many schools; I took the Marriage Counseling Course. I didn't know what would work or how to do it, but **I just kept taking action.**

I was frustrated when I was turned down by so many schools, but I just kept going. **Persistence** is so very important. A lot of people stop when they hit a road block, or they try something and it doesn't feel good. You just need to take one step after another, even though you certainly can't know the whole plan.

We'll get more in depth on these ideas in this book. As you follow the directions in this book, you'll find your life opening up many more possibilities for you. **Remember, as parents handle their own stress related problems, the jobs of parenting and work become easier and are handled better.**

Success Begins with the Decision to Succeed

Deciding WHAT you want isn't enough. You need to go out there and **take action** to succeed. Start by writing an action plan. It may require hard work on your part, but you must move forward. I have discovered a universal truth: *People who feel good about their goals, and who have made the decision to succeed, take action to attract the success that they desire.*

EXERCISE: Take that first step by asking yourself:

"What would I do with my life if _____ was no longer an issue?"
"How would my life be different?"
"What would I be doing that's different? "

The answers to these questions will motivate you to continue through the challenge.

You can propel forward by making some of these changes a reality even before you achieve your goal. For example, one woman who wanted to lose weight said that on achieving her goal, she would buy a red dress. I suggested she buy that red dress now. One woman who wanted to get into a good relationship said, if she did, she would do more nice things for herself. Her assignment was to do something nice for herself every day, starting now.

You need to take action now. Saying and believing your affirmations is not enough for abundance to flow from the skies. It does not matter whether you know all the steps you eventually will need to take. You start from where you are.

Perhaps this means that you join a group, put an ad on the Internet, or put an exercise class in your schedule. As you take the first small step, more ideas will come to your mind about the next few steps. What is important is that you have written your plan down, and are now generating energy around achieving this goal. This partial plan you have is not written in stone. You will modify it as you go along.

There may be times when some of your actions do not work out, and you feel discouraged. If you are looking for a great relationship, you may need to utilize a lot of creative energy meeting many potential partners. If you are looking for a great job, there may be failed interviews. If you are trying to reach a certain weight goal, eating a piece of chocolate cake is not a complete failure. Instead look at the many days in which you succeeded staying away from chocolate. You can learn from each experience.

The most successful people make the most mistakes. But they don't make the same mistake twice. **Don't be afraid to make mistakes. Don't harshly judge yourself when you make mistakes. Just learn from them.**

Take that first step. Write as much of your action plan as you can write today. Continue working on your plan, making the necessary adjustments. Your plan is a "plan in motion," and it is an essential step in turning your success goal into a success reality.

Chapter 5

Don't Be Afraid to Change Direction

We decide on a goal and become quite eager to achieve it. But enthusiasm soon wanes. Why?

Although we all have something (or many things) in our life that we would like to change, we experience a lot of difficulty making a permanent change. We might decide to start exercising every day. We join a gym and for a few days we go after work. Then one day a friend calls and says, "Let's have a drink and dinner after work." It's only one day and so we forget the gym.

Then the next day we're tired and excuse ourselves from the gym. We might go the next day. The following day we need to work overtime. Then we need to go shopping after work. Then we think it might be easier to go before work. We wake up early a couple of days. But we're too sleepy and turn the alarm on snooze. Soon mornings are impossible. You get the picture. We're not going to the gym anymore.

Why is it so hard to change? Why do we not go to the gym even though we know how important exercise is and are very upset about our weight and the fat on our bodies? It's painful and yet we remain the same. And though it's more painful to feel fat then to go to the gym, we still don't change.

The next question to ask yourself is, "How will I sabotage this plan?" You already know that you've sabotaged previous plans. One of the ways that people sabotage themselves is by planning to make too many changes simultaneously.

What Needs to Happen for Us to Make a Change?

We need to ask ourselves what is needed to make a change. What is practical for us? Be honest with yourself. You've already done a lot of talking about it, but haven't really continued with your goals. Perhaps it isn't a membership at the gym. Perhaps walking at lunchtime would better fit your schedule. Write down your answer and do some long, hard thinking about it.

Perhaps you've attempted too much all at once. Perhaps you're suddenly worried about how others will perceive your success. Will your family and friends be happy for you, or will they disapprove and perhaps desert you? Do you have some unconscious beliefs that you're not worthy or deserving of success? Is a part of you afraid of change? These fears have stopped a lot of people from making a change. **As parents handle their own stress related problems, the jobs of parenting and work become easier and are handled better.**

Fear of Change

"Fear of change" is one of the most powerful fears. No matter how much we want things to change, often it is easier to stay within our own "circle of comfort." We may not like where we are, but at least it is familiar. We do not know what it will be like if we change.

Fears about change include:

"I'm afraid to change."
"They won't like me if I change."
"Success can be very scary."
"This is all anybody expects of me."
"I don't want to rock the boat."
"I don't know how to handle success."
"All my friends also have this problem. Why be different?"
"It's easier to stay where I am. At least I know what to expect."
"It's too hard to try to achieve my goal."

These fears can apply universally to all goals, from relationships to professional success. Even people who are successful in many areas of their lives may still have one area where they are afraid of change. Many people are unaware that they have a belief system that is interfering with their success. Unless we neutralize our negative underlying beliefs, any gains realized will be short lived.

If you are having difficulty in one area of your life, try this: Stand in front of a mirror and say the above "fear of change" statements out loud. If any of the statements cause an emotional reaction within you, that could be a hint that you are getting close to a limiting belief.

EXERCISE:

Make the following empowering statements in front of a mirror or with a friend. Notice again how you feel. Make a note of any area that you are not comfortable saying. These are empowering statements that are difficult to say if you don't believe in them. Examples of empowering beliefs are:

"I enjoy change and growth."
"My friends (relatives, co-workers) are happy to see me succeed."
"Success feels very good."
"I love realizing my potential."
"I deserve to have _____ (what I want)."
"I can be safe having _____ (what I want)."

EXERCISE:

Many clients have found this exercise to be very revealing of their negativity. Wear a rubber band around your wrist and pay attention to your negative thoughts—the Inner Critical Voice discussed earlier—that you have during the day. Every time you think a negative thought, snap the rubber band. You will learn how to stop thinking negative thoughts by making them more conscious.

As a working mom, you need to be careful that you are not making too many immediate goals. Women still do most of the care taking of children, the housework, the making of appointments, and other tasks. Perhaps because women are more suited to caretaking than men, it has always fallen on their shoulders. Even in an equalitarian relationship, the burden is much stronger for women. The women who seem to be Super Moms are often the women who have incomes that allow them to hire housekeepers and nannies. If you have the salary of a social worker or a teacher, or perhaps you make a minimum wage, you need to take this in consideration.

Perhaps there are a few years, when children are very young, that you need to take time out from a career. Or you might have a part time job. Christina worked half time, but found that she was working more than twenty hours a week because she had so many assignments. Janet, a highly successful saleswoman, is doing some job sharing with another mother. They share all leads and clients. They each work two days and on alternate Wednesdays. You might consider working at home although it is extremely difficult with children always interrupting you. And if you need to work to be able to pay the bills, just realize and give yourself credit that you are doing a Herculean task.

Nevertheless, there can be positive changes that can be made to your life. As you lower your stress level (ability you will achieve by learning the tapping that I introduce later in this chapter), you can accomplish more and enjoy your life more. You can learn to get over any guilt that you may have over not accomplishing as much (or as fast) as someone who doesn't have children. You can enjoy more time with your spouse and children.

Learn to have smaller short term goals within a larger long term goal. How will I celebrate reaching my goal? Be sure to celebrate all the successes—big or small.

EXERCISE:

As you think of your goal what will you look like? What will you see in others? What will you be saying? What will others say to you? Do not be satisfied by just saying you'll feel good.

Chapter 6

Get Out of That Overwhelm Trap

Do you feel stuck? Overstressed? Overwhelmed?

Do you feel like no matter how hard you try to make changes in your life, something always keeps that from happening? Are you struggling to lose weight, enjoy a good relationship with a partner, or start a new adventure in your life? Life has a way of overwhelming us, with to-dos, problems, and circumstances.

What I have discovered is that when we are overwhelmed, we become paralyzed, and then we put off the actions we need to take to reach our dreams and goals.

The information on these pages can help you overcome overwhelm and get you into your flow and into your go! It is not a miracle cure and it will take practice. You can live a life of significance, purpose, passion, and fulfillment.

Part of being overwhelmed is the feeling that you have too much to do, too many tasks to complete to accomplish any goal. Joan was thinking of the things she needed to do to launch her business program. She had to get a website, draw up the curriculum, get a webinar ready, figure out the marketing, and do the sales. Then she had to stop work every night at 5:00 p.m. to get dinner ready for the family. She couldn't do anything and she just froze. She sought some help from me. We wrote down the steps she needed to take and then prioritized them. Then she set about doing one thing at a time. It's very important to break down a big project into smaller steps on a to-do list. You can check off completed tasks and have a sense of completion almost every day.

Mary had two small children, a husband working full time, a big house, and she was taking courses at a community college so that she could get a degree. She never found time to study because the house was so big and her husband was a perfectionist in wanting it kept clean and neat, in addition to attending to her children and making good dinners. After working with me, she realized that part of her overwhelm was caused by repressed anger with her husband's criticism. She resolved the anger issues with tapping and by clear communication with her husband. Now her husband cooks several nights and is not so fussy about messiness.

Sharon was a people pleaser. She completely avoided confrontation with anyone including her husband, coworkers, and children. The president of the PTA begged her to head the committee for the fundraising bakery sale. The week before the fundraiser, her boss was going out of town for two weeks and wanted Sharon to take over and do the final accounting ledger for the last quarter. Her husband got a sinus infection and didn't have the energy to help with the cooking or handling the children's dinner and bedtime. Sharon felt ragged and exhausted, but didn't know how to say "No" or ask for help. "This always happens to me. I need to take over when other people don't do the job, even though I'm exhausted." She complained that she couldn't say "No" because then people would think she was mean and she wants to make people happy. She felt beaten down by all of things she "should" do, but just really couldn't.

Overwhelm can be caused by not knowing what steps to take or by unexpressed (and often unrealized) emotions. Joan had to learn that you can only start from where you are. Sometimes you need coaching or counseling to learn the correct steps to take and in what order. And then you need to take small steps one at a time to accomplish your goals. The key is to take action—small steps at a time—not an immediate leap.

Mary had to learn that sometimes feeling overwhelmed is a way of the body telling you that you need to handle certain unresolved emotions before you can take action. She had to handle her anger and learn how to communicate clearly. Sharon had to work on childhood abuse that she experienced. She then learned how to stand up for herself and how to say "No" and feel fine about it. A later chapter goes into more detail about the ability to say "No!"

There are many books, webinars, and classes that tell you how to do something. But if you know what to do and you aren't doing it, the problem is probably emotional. This is where EFT can help you heal these emotions. It is important to know that understanding "why" you act the way you do is not usually sufficient. You need a **healing of the emotions.**

Whether you are looking to move up in the business world, save your marriage, pull yourself out of depression, lose weight or quit smoking, or just overcome excess stress and overwhelm, these tools will help you find the "Overcomer" inside of you and stomp those bad habits into the ground.

EXERCISE:

1. When did the feeling of stress and overwhelm start?
2. What was happening in your life at the time?
3. How do you stabilize or calm yourself when you get stressed? List all the ways.
4. Do you have recurring memories or nightmares that won't go away?
5. If there is a chronic physical pain, ask yourself, "If there is an emotional issue associated with this condition, what might it be?"

PART II

DISCOVER THE POWER OF EFT (TAPPING)

Chapter 7

Working with EFT (Learn How This Centuries-Old Technique Can Transform Your Life)

The concept behind Emotional Freedom Techniques (EFT) also known as tapping, is a modern application based on the Chinese acupuncture technique of energy points discovered about 5,000 years ago. Integrating the ancient wisdoms of the past with modern therapies of today, tapping is becoming a successful western application, producing happier and healthier lifestyles. Today we are being challenged daily with stress, panic, anger, anxiety, cravings, and other negative emotions that block our energy systems and end up disrupting our quality of life. These negative emotions easily manifest into physical problems. We feel nervous in our stomachs, stress in our shoulders, or fear in our sweaty palms. Tapping releases these blocked energies to allow both emotional and physical healing to occur.

EFT is so effective because it recognizes the unity of the body/mind connection. It lowers the stress level (specifically the cortisol and adrenaline hormones) so that you do not have to go through a lot of emotional pain to achieve an emotional breakthrough. In fact, part of its effectiveness is that as you evolve into understanding what is going on internally, you may probably smile and say, "It does seem silly, doesn't it?" You can take a step back and then realize that you made the best decision possible as a child. You don't have to stick with that decision as an adult. It identifies and heals the root causes of the issues in our life that continue to sabotage us year after year—and sometimes decade after decade.

How EFT Works

By tapping on specific areas, and by repeating key words, the nature of the pain is acknowledged and then finally accepted. The trapped emotions are released, and the body begins to heal as new thoughts and new patterns become rewired in the brain.

During this process, hidden, but related, emotions can often arise signaling to the body a need to be healed. Thinking of a painful incident sends stress messages to the brain. The tapping gives the message to the brain to lower the stress level. The brain is getting conflicting messages. Eventually the tapping wins and you can think of the previously painful event without the pain because the brain has been rewired. You do not forget an incident, but you just react differently. You are free from the emotional attachment to this incident.

Below is the diagram for tapping points.

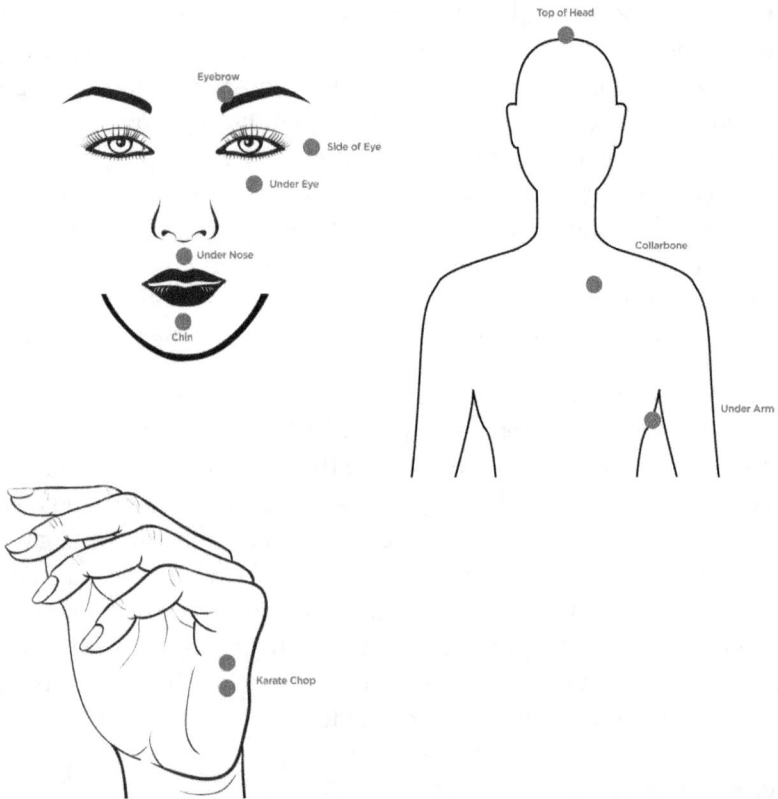

First you think of an incident that you wish to tap on. It's important to be as specific here as possible. Then attach an emotion to that incident and assign a numeric level to that pain of 1 to 10, where 10 is the worst pain you can imagine, and 0 is no pain. Write down the emotion and the numeric intensity.

Notice if there is any sensation in your body as you think of this incident. If so, describe this sensation in as much detail as possible. Then give a numeric level to this sensation. (Again we measure the intensity of the sensation from 1 to 10, with 10 being the most intense.) As we practice more, I will be asking you to remember the earliest time of your life when you recall feeling this sensation. Many emotional situations have physical symptoms that crop up over and over. Oftentimes, a current problem is solved by handling childhood issues. It is important to write down the intensity level because as the emotional or physical pain subsides, people often don't remember how severe the pain was. They are amazed that in a matter of minutes, pain which has been bothering them, perhaps for decades, can be reduced so quickly.

One of the questions that I am frequently asked is why do we have to include the negative? People tell me that, "We should try and be positive and only make positive statements." You need to be able to be honest with yourself and see what the problem is before you can correct it. It's like cleaning the cobwebs from the window so you can see the light. Saying the problem is essential for the set-up statement.

When you are tapping, tap each point about 5 to 7 times. It is not a hard tap where you hurt or bruise yourself. It is not a light feathery touch. It is a firm touch. (I think of Goldilocks and the three bears. It is not too hot and not too cold, but just right.)

1st Round of Tapping

1. Issue/feeling or problem I need to work on: Use 3 or 4 words to give a name to the problem.
2. My set-up statement: Tapping starts with a set-up statement that acknowledges the problem by focusing attention on the emotion or event that activates the negative energy: "Even though I have this problem, I deeply and completely love and accept myself." If you can't say you love and accept yourself, you might say something such as, "I hope to someday love and accept myself." You tap on the Karate Chop point (the side of the hand) for these statements.
3. My reminder phrases: Here you are repeating the problem but using only a few words. "I'm angry, I'm overwhelmed." You'll also notice in the following sample scripts that I added further statements about feelings. For these statements you are using all of the alternate tapping points in the diagram.

4. Intensity of emotion(s) felt: On a scale of 1 to 10 with 10 being the most intense, what number best describes you?

5. Physical sensations felt: As you scan your body, you might notice tightness or other sensations in your body. Describe in as much detail as possible. Include size of area, shape, temperature, steady or pulsating.

6. Intensity level of physical sensation: Again use the scale of 1 to 10, with 10 being the most intense.

We start with the karate chop point. This is on the side of the hand. You tap it lightly stating the problem 3 times, along with a positive statement such as, "I completely love and accept myself." Then we tap on either side with either hand. It doesn't make any difference which side we tap on, but some people will eventually feel like one side is stronger than the other.

You repeatedly tap on the problem until you get the intensity level down to a 3 or lower. It is only after you can lower the intensity level down to that 3 or lower that you can use the positive statements. People who have been accustomed to only talk about the positive, often ask why they need to talk about the problem. The answer is that you need to start with where you are before you can move forward. You need to see the lint on your glasses, before you can clean them off.

Let's keep tapping until we got that intensity level down. If you cannot get it down, it may be that you have bumped into a deeper problem than you at first realized. Get some help from an experienced practitioner if this happens to you.

2nd Round of Tapping: Notice the same things you noticed in 1st Round.

3rd Round of Tapping

4th Round of Tapping

5th Round of Tapping

Chapter 8

Tap Out That Stress and Keep Moving Forward

Some Additional EFT Tapping Tips

- Use your own language.

- Write down in your own words how you feel. (You can pretend you're talking to your best friend on the telephone.)

- Tapping can be done with either (or both) hands on either side of the body.

- Always write down the name of the incident and the intensity level.

- Many stresses can be worked on your own. However, if there is an increase in the intensity level or there is a serious trauma, it is better to work with a qualified practitioner.

EXERCISE:

Here are three different tapping scripts to start you off on tapping. You can use these scripts verbatim, mix and match lines, or use your own specific language.

When tapping, tap on each point 5 to 7 times. Tap lightly enough so that you are not sore later. You should be saying these words out loud. Remember that you can substitute your own words in any of these scripts.

Script #1

Karate Chop Point: "Even though I am under a lot of stress combining motherhood and a career, I deeply love and accept myself." (Repeat words 3 times.)

Top of Head: "So much stress."

Eyebrow: "Tired all the time."

Side of Eye: "Don't have much energy."

Under Eye: "Too much to do."

Under Nose: "Never have a minute to myself."

Chin: "Doesn't feel like I'm a good mother."

Collarbone: "Why can't I be Super Mom?"

Under Arm: "I feel so guilty."

Top of Head: "This is impossible."

Eyebrow: "Why is it so hard?"

Side of Eye: "Doing poorly at work."

Under Eye: "Other women do it."

Under Nose: "So guilty."

Chin: "So incompetent."

Collarbone: "So tired."

Under Arm: "Why can't I be Super Mom?"

When (and if) you get your intensity level down to a 3 or less, you might tap on the following round. Don't worry if you don't get to it.

Top of Head: "Maybe there's another way to look at this. Maybe I'm trying to do an impossible job."

Eyebrow: "This is really a difficult job. This isn't my imagination."

Side of Eye: "Maybe I need to give myself credit for all that I am accomplishing."

Under Eye: "I still need to do most of the childhood caring and household tasks."

Under Nose: "Super Mom is just a myth."

Chin: "I will get some support for myself."

Collarbone: "I am doing the best that I can."

Under Arm: "I can lower my stress level so that I enjoy motherhood more."

Script #2

Karate Chop Point: "Even though I feel pressured to act right now, I deeply and completely love and accept myself." (EFT set-up phrase. Say 3 times.)

Eyebrow: "I feel the pressure to act right now."

Side of Eye: "I feel so anxious and need to do something now."

Under Eye: "I feel compelled to act now."

Under Nose: "I feel so agitated about this issue."

Chin: "I don't think I should wait."

Collarbone: "I am very stressed out right now."

Underarm: "Shouldn't I do something about this situation?"

Top of Head: "I feel so urgent about this problem."

Gamut Point: "Now for the positive focus on problem." *(Make sure your intensity level is 3 or less before you say the positive statements.)*

Eyebrow: "I choose to feel peaceful before I take action."

Side of Eye: "I want to feel relaxed and at peace before I act."

Under Eye: "I intend to feel peaceful about this conflict."

Under Nose: "I appreciate how relaxed I can feel even though I have this problem."

Chin: "I love feeling so relaxed and calm."

Collarbone: "Thank you, universe, for the creative guidance about this."

Under arm: "I am ready to enjoy the peace and quiet in my mind."

Top of Head: "I appreciate the wisdom that is coming to me."

Tap on following phrases as you complete another round:

"I love knowing we all deserve abundance."

"I choose to believe in the guidance I am receiving."

"I appreciate the prosperity in my life."

"I love appreciating my body, my friends, my opportunities."

"I'm grateful for all the new opportunities for abundance."

"I appreciate exactly who I am."

"I appreciate all the lessons I have learned."

"I am so grateful for all the prosperity in my life."

Script # 3

Gamut Point: "Even though I feel like I don't know the exact action steps to take for my life, I deeply and completely love and accept myself." (Set-up phrase.)

Top of Head: "Nothing has seemed to work so far."

Eyebrow: "I've tried everything I can think of."

Side of Eye: "It's very frustrating and disappointing."

Under Eye: "Why doesn't it work?"

Under Nose: "Every time I try to do something, I feel _____ in my body."

Chin: "Every time I think that I deserve to have _____, I hear a judgmental voice inside of me saying, _____."

Collarbone: "I just feel like I can't be successful."

Under Arm: "Why does it have to be so hard?"

Top of Head: "It just seems impossible to have _____."

Eyebrow: "I might as well give up."

Side of Eye: "I just feel so hopeless."

Under Eye: "It's so frustrating and disappointing."

Under Nose: "Nothing ever seems to work."

Chin: "Why can't I do (or have) this?"

Collarbone: "I've tried everything I can think of, but nothing works."

Under Arm: "Nothing works."

When you get to an intensity of 1, 2, or 3, you can do the next round of tapping.

Top of Head: "I am open to discovering new possibilities."

Eyebrow: "I am willing to listen to my emotions instead of trying to push them down."

Side of Eye: "I'm going to be willing to examine my beliefs about success."

Under Eye: "I'm going to be willing to do whatever it takes to overcome events and patterns from my past that don't serve me."

Under Nose: "I am committed to my growth."

Chin: "I will find the courage to overcome myself doubts and fears."

Collarbone: "If necessary, I'm willing to fail many times, because I know that in the end I will be successful."

Under Arm: "I will learn to do the important things first instead of the easy things."

Top of Head: "I can get clear on what I want and who I want to be."

Eyebrow: "I will take daily action to get where I want to be."

Side of Eye: "As I learn more and more about myself, I will be feeling more and more like I deserve success and I will achieve success!"

This tapping releases the stress hormone, cortisol, and can be used alone or with words.

If you get stuck at any intensity rating for several rounds, ask yourself whether something else has come up or something else is coming up that you need to focus on.

Sometimes you may think that you are tapping on a relatively simple issue, but when you tap, some other incident or stronger emotion pops up. This may be a signal that you are venturing into sensitive territory and you may want to tap with an experienced practitioner.

It is also helpful for a mother of a very young child to tap on the child or, when the child is a little older, to teach him to tap. The words will be simpler. Instead of saying, "I completely love and accept myself." The child can say, "I am a good boy." Or "I'm an OK boy." This is best done as a game between parent and child.

When children are a little older, it might be fun to tap together as a family. Or children might want to tap on a doll.

EXERCISE: 10 Incidents That Annoyed You_

This exercise will help you get into the habit of tapping. Write down 10 incidents that annoyed you. (We are not talking about extreme anger—only annoyance.) For each incident that you come up with do the following exercise.

1. Imagine the incident vividly.
2. Bring in as many of the five senses that you can.
3. Feel the emotion.

Feel the body location where you experience this. Describe it in detail. A pain might be throbbing, steady, or like a knife wound. There might be a temperature in that part of the body. Maybe there's tension in certain areas, or the pain has a shape and size, maybe a color.

Now remember the first time you felt that **physical** feeling **in your body.** Remember the incident if possible. Early age feelings may not come with an incident. Give the incident a name.

Now think back in time do when you had that same bodily feeling. Give the event a name. The event should be something that took about 3 minutes in actual time. There might be several incidents in that short time frame. Tap on each one until you get the intensity number down to a 1 or 2. Then go to the next incident. If this incident has several emotions attached, get each emotion down to a level 2 or 3 before going on to the next emotion. If you think of several events, take the earliest one and tap on it.

Tap on each item from the exercise in the following sequence until you get the intensity down. If this gets too difficult, you may need to work with an experienced tapper.

- Issue/Feeling or Problem I need to work with.

- My set-up statement

- My reminder phrases

- Beginning intensity level for emotion and intensity level for physical sensation (1 to 10).

- Tap on the event. You may need to do 5 rounds.

- What is the ending emotional and physical intensity level?

Go on to the next incident until you have done this for all 10 events.

Is there any recurring emotion or body sensation? Think of some mistakes that you make over and over. Is there any relationship that you see between mistakes and the emotions and incidents that you have experienced in this tapping? As you think about this, it makes your obstacles even clearer.

As parents handle their own stress related problems, the jobs of parenting and work become easier and are handled better.

PART III

OVERCOME THE OBSTACLES
THAT HOLD YOU BACK!

Chapter 9

Feel Like, "I Deserve to Reach My Goals!"

Your goal in reading this book may be to lower the stress level of combining motherhood with a career. This book is specializing in this combination, but you may also have separate parenthood goals or career goals. This exercise is good for any of these goals. You have had these goals for a while, but something seems to be getting in the way of your succeeding at accomplishing them. This chapter is going to pinpoint the obstacles that stand in your way. The next chapters explain how to get rid of these obstacles.

Besides lowering the stress level that you are experiencing, you may have other big goals. Perhaps it's earning a certain amount of money or to be promoted to a certain position in the company, or to have your own business, or be a part-time business woman and a part-time mother. Perhaps you would like to have a better relationship with your spouse. Or if you're a single mother, perhaps you would enjoy having a fulfilling relationship.

Should you have other goals or should you just be satisfied with being a mother and working? Do you have guilty feelings because you want to do and be more than a working mother? Are you beating yourself up because you want more in your life? Or are your children now old enough so that you feel you can devote more time to success on a career, but somehow you don't move forward? This next exercise can help you identify specific beliefs that stop you from moving forward and cause you a lot of stress.

EXERCISE:

Imagine that you are on the stage in an auditorium with 100 people in the audience. These people include those from today and from the past. Include your parents, children, other important family members, the people you work with, important teachers from your education, religious leaders, neighbors and anyone else who has been or is now important in your life.

Now imagine yourself in front of the audience with a big sign declaring, "I've succeeded in my goal!" In a loud clear voice, declare to the audience that you have already achieved this goal and it is much more impressive than even you dreamed. Look them in their eyes as you confidently express this statement.

Pause and pay attention to your feelings now. Look at the audience.

Take out your journal or a separate piece of paper. Answer the following questions about this goal.

1. What was the emotion that you felt when you declared your victory to the audience? Did you feel the same way for each person you declared it to? On a scale of 1 to 10, with 10 being the most intense, what number is it?

3. What did you physically experience in your body when you declared your victory? What number is it?

4. What did you see on the faces of the people in the audience? What was the most negative emotion that showed? Did any of the audience turn their backs on you?

5. Did you hear any inner voice criticizing you or arguing with you? What did it say?

6. Was there some childhood rule about boasting or achieving something that you just broke? If so, what is the rule?

7. Do you have an unconscious expectation that people will react this way to any success you might achieve?

8. Is there a part of you that automatically starts to say over and over to yourself what you remember hearing from others in your past?

9. Are you aware how much this might have cost you in the last 5 years? (physically, emotionally and financially)?

I Deserve

What happened to you when you thought of your goal? Let's start with the statement, "I deserve to have _____." What emotion did it bring up?

What happens in your body when you say, "I deserve to have_____."

I hope this exercise made you aware of some belief that you have that is perhaps holding you back. Remember in the Introduction of this book how I discussed my decision that it was not safe for me to share who I really am? Maybe you have just stated or heard a voice from the audience sharing something similar—something that has been holding you back from achieving your goal.

Chapter 10

Escape the Frozen Weather of Trauma and PTSD (Post Traumatic Stress Disorder)

I am including this information on PTSD (post-traumatic stress disorder) because so many women have been molested as a child or grown up in a dysfunctional family. PTSD is not something that only happens to veterans. When parents suffer from PTSD, this affects the parenting of children, as well as how the parent acts in the workplace and with friends and relatives. If a woman and her children are living with an individual who has PTSD, they too could suffer. Until there is healing, there can be no change. Talking alone is not enough. When processing past traumas, it is important to work with an experienced counselor. This work is too emotionally fraught to do this on your own. Be aware that living with a parent who has PTSD often causes the spouse and children to suffer with PTSD.

Fight, Flight, or Freeze

Whenever a person gets triggered or activated by traumatic memories, or other visceral experiences, the prefrontal cortex shuts down and the limbic brain (e.g., the emotional brain) takes over. Just talking can activate the emotional brain, but just talking is not likely to shut it down.

A distressing event is characterized as a "trauma" when we experience two features—both a threat to our survival and extreme helplessness. When you experience a trauma, your system "freezes" because the terror is too overwhelming to process at that moment.

An extreme example of trauma is when some veterans have PTSD (post-traumatic stress disorder). They may feel guilty about surviving when their close friend next to them was killed. Perhaps they sent someone on a mission and that person was killed. Or perhaps they killed an approaching child who was carrying a bomb. Or they looked at the bodies of those they killed. It has been very difficult for some veterans to let go of their guilt. Women who live with men who have PTSD have also developed PTSD. With more women entering the armed forces, the services are finding out that many women have been sexually harassed, also resulting in PTSD.

Two results are inevitable: 1) These sensations—sights, sounds, and smells—are stored in our bodies' memories; and, 2) They will resurface at another time. When you are deprived of an opportunity to discharge the physical and emotional repercussions of the original trauma, the unresolved feelings are expressed through flashbacks, intense arousal, avoidance, or other problematic behaviors every day.

A major feature of trauma is the distortion of memory that occurs as a safety mechanism to protect us from being overwhelmed.

EFT addresses the whole brain by sending out soothing hormones, while at the same time talking about the trauma. You are holding the experience and discomfort in the body at the same time that you are relaxed and calm. Two competing emotions are sent to the brain and the brain eventually accepts the more calming message.

The ACES (Adverse Childhood Experiences) study was conducted by Kaiser Permanente with over 17,000 patients. The object was to discover if early childhood experiences had any effect on adults. They looked at ten different types of experience: Physical abuse, emotional abuse, sexual abuse, physical neglect, emotional neglect, household dysfunction from mental illness, mother treated violently, divorce, one or more ACES. The more ACES there were, the greater risk for behavioral, physical, and mental health problems. Of the 17,000 patients, 64% had at least one ACE.

The behaviors included lack of physical activities, alcoholism, smoking, drug use, and missed work. Physical and mental health issues included severe obesity, diabetes, depression, suicide attempts, STDs, heart disease, cancer, stroke, COPD, and broken bones. Some people carried these effects 50 years after childhood.

When we face a trauma, what really matters is how we react to it. People who have been in car accidents may be afraid to drive certain places, or at night, or perhaps all the time. People who have been shamed by an elementary school teacher in front of a class may start perspiring when they are assigned a public presentation. People who have been turned down for a date when they were young teenagers may fear rejection as adults.

Women who have been raped may distrust all men. Adults who have been abused as a child may find it impossible to achieve their goals.

The ACES study proved that individuals suffer from early childhood experiences. This is often carried on from generation to generation. Perhaps you've heard how certain families have generational repetitions of alcoholics, drug addiction, or depressives in their families.

The ACES study is what is sometimes referred to as big "T" traumas. Then there are the little "t" traumas. Being told that money doesn't grow on trees is a small "t" trauma, but it is the kind of issue that gets in the way of achieving financial success as an adult. It is also a belief system that gets passed down in generations.

What happens is that you get a gut wrenching reaction to certain events or places. You then say or do something that you didn't intend. Or perhaps you just freeze and can't respond. Logically you know something, but you act as if you don't know or believe. As shown in the story of my high school trauma (in the Introduction), I froze and couldn't talk about myself to those that were close to me. I just didn't feel safe. I didn't connect it in my mind to those high school years until I did some tapping.

Tom, a veteran from the Iraqi war, was ready to go out celebrating. There was a new Mexican restaurant in town and he wanted to try out the chili rellenos. He sat down and ordered a beer to go with the meal. The smells were so inviting and he eagerly awaited his food. Suddenly he heard a loud crash. Immediately he was back in Iraq and he dove for shelter under the table. After a few minutes he realized that the crash was from a busboy who had accidentally dropped the dishes. Embarrassed he slinked out of the restaurant without waiting to eat. Like many PTSD victims with a big "T" trauma, he hurtled back in time and reacted as if he was still in that dangerous situation. Tom was divorced and not in any relationship.

Gerry was driving one rainy night in San Diego when a gusty wind started. The rain fell harder and harder as she was crossing over the Coronado Bridge. She grasped the steering wheel tightly and felt a nervous feeling in her stomach. Her breathing became shallow. She momentarily lost control and although she wasn't hurt and nothing happened to the car, she has avoided that bridge for 20 years.

Jessie was singing as she put on her best green dress. At age 17 she was going on her first date with Jim, a good looking young man of 21 that she had just met. He had his own car and was going to take her to the movies and then for a bite to eat. She smiled as she got in his car thinking that this was one of the most exciting nights of her life. Instead of going to the movie theater he drove to a lonely field. He reached across to kiss her and she was surprised. Suddenly he thrust her down in the seat of the car and raped her. Then he drove her home and warned her not to tell anybody. "They won't believe you anyway." She was stunned. She didn't dare tell anyone about it. "After all, it's my fault for not knowing that I shouldn't trust him." She blamed herself for not knowing better. Twenty-five years later she still blames herself when anything bad happens to her—even though she wasn't responsible. This was a big "T" trauma that negatively affected her for those 25 years. I was the first person she told about the incident because of her shame. She also shared that her daughter was shy and didn't take chances.

Julie was in a car accident where her car was totaled. Even though she didn't get hurt, she felt anxiety when she was driving. When she finally realized that she was safe in a car, she no longer felt anxiety when driving. Because she was a very resilient person, this was a little "t" trauma and the anxiety was released with a few group therapy sessions.

After an event in which we feel helpless and threatened (as in some of the above examples), people make decisions about their world and what is safe. They may not even remember the actual situation, but the memory is in their brain and body and they react to the current situation as if they were in the past. The important thing is that their reactions are oftentimes an attempt to protect themselves. They need a healing to lower the stress level and be more productive and a better parent.

The important thing to understand is that what is traumatic to one person may not be traumatic to another. Whether it's a small trauma little "t" or a big actual life threatening big "T" trauma, when we feel helpless and threatened, we encode the memory in our brain and body. We may or may not consciously remember the incident, but major life changing decisions are often made as a result.

Do you have an area of your life where you don't feel safe and logically it seems irrational? People can be triggered into a feeling of anxiety or fear by many kinds of situations. Perhaps a smell can remind someone of some terrible incident. A certain look by someone can trigger a feeling of helplessness as they flash back to when Dad gave them that look. Perhaps someone has a certain way of walking that reminds you of another person. A piece of music can remind you of a feeling. Although there can be many different triggers, people will feel a certain emotion—yet they won't necessarily connect it to a traumatic memory.

Are there certain areas of your life where you get tense or perhaps don't want to do something? You may be reacting to an unconscious trigger? Although you may not have experienced these exact same situations, everybody has some situations that have caused them stress. You may even find yourself reacting in a knee jerk reaction like the way your mother did after a trauma she experienced. And, yes, your children will react the way that you did after a trauma you experienced.

If you are suffering from PTSD it is best to get the help of an experienced EFT practitioner. You are not only helping yourself, but you are helping your children.

Chapter 11

Banish the Resistance to Change

"I just think I could change if only John would do _____, or my boss was more understanding, or my kids were better behaved, or _____." It's so easy to blame outside influences for being stuck where we are. I've heard many people say, "I've started to follow the suggestions in the book, and then life gets in the way."

Denise stated that she was waiting for the "right time" to start on her project. After her boss hired another worker, and her husband got a raise, and the children got better grades in school, then she could consider starting.

Jane told me that she had tried to be more assertive. Her children were very happy that she would be more assertive with her coworkers. When it came time for Jane to be assertive with her children about picking up their mess, she found out that they became very angry with her. "I hate you!" they shouted. They messed up the house even more and screamed at her. She felt that the children were sabotaging all her efforts.

Unfortunately, there is never a right time to make a deep lasting change. Life will always get in the way. Life happens to all of us. Family and a lot of close friends say they are happy, and yet they often fight hard to keep the current state. They don't want **YOU** to change the way that you act with them, just with other people.

Another fear of change is that we won't know ourselves if we change. Perhaps all our friends and family will leave us and we'll be all alone. Maybe they'll look down on us.

There is a fear of change no matter how hard we want a different outcome. A lot of time we don't realize we have this fear. It's easier to blame outside circumstances and people. It is important to realize as we talk about change that we cannot change other people. We can only change ourselves. The good news is that as we no longer react in our old habitual ways, and act in different ways, others can no longer react to us in the old way. They also will change—sometimes in the way that you would want them to change, and sometimes in other ways. There is no guarantee.

As we go into this next exercise think of an issue in your life you wish to change. Pick an issue that you have been trying unsuccessfully to change. Perhaps a part of you is experiencing a resistance to change. Let's explore!

EXERCISE:

Think of the change resistant part of you. Where in your body do you experience it? Is there tension anywhere in your body? Are there any temperature changes? Is your breathing changing? As you think of this, what is your intensity level?

Karate Chop: (Set-up statement) "Even though I feel quite resistant to change, I deeply and completely love and accept myself."

Top of Head: "This part of me cannot change."

Eyebrow: "Change is too difficult."

Side of Eye: "Change is impossible."

Under Eye: "I can't change my life."

Under Nose: "I can't change other people."

Chin: "I'm just going to stay stuck my whole life."

Collarbone: "Nobody can help me."

Under Arm: "I don't know why it's so difficult."

Go through this several times until you get the intensity level to 3 or less.

Top of Head: "Maybe it will be possible to change."

Eyebrow: "I wonder if it's possible to be easy to change."

Side of Eye: "I can learn how to change."

Under Eye: "Maybe it will be easy to change."

Chin: "As I gather the courage, I will be able to change."

Collarbone: "I can change whatever I want to change in my behavior."

Under Arm: "Even if I don't change I will love and accept myself anyway."

Chapter 12

Break Free from Perfectionism

Perfectionism is something that applies to only some people. Skip over this section is you are not a perfectionist.

Perfectionists have the feeling that they are *not good enough*, that they are *inadequate*, they feel they need to *do more*, and they *must have the highest standards.* They have impossible standards and they use their performance to make them feel better. They will use their behavior to control people around them.

If you are a perfectionist, you will usually **overwork** without enough rest. You are always **dissatisfied**. You want to make sure that you **do not make mistakes**. You are **never doing enough**. There is a lot **anxiety** since you are always careful and making sure there are no mistakes. Sometimes you **procrastinate**. This perfectionism gets in the way of happiness, success, and intimacy. After all, it is impossible to be perfect.

As a mother, do you feel guilty because you're not the perfect mother? What do you think will happen to you if you are not perfect? Are you trying to raise the perfect child? What if you were exhausted and screamed at your children one night? Are you afraid that they will suffer for the rest of their life?

Luckily for us we can tell children we made a mistake. We can apologize to our child if we shouted at them. We can even have a discussion with our children about how everyone makes mistakes. Hopefully we learn from our mistakes and don't make the same mistake twice.

EXERCISE: *Tapping Script for Perfectionism*

(Remember, you can substitute your own words)

Karate Chop: "Even though I'm afraid of falling short because I'm not good enough (or inadequate or not perfect), I deeply and completely love and accept myself." (Repeat 3 times.)

Top of Head: "I don't think I'm enough"

Eyebrow: "I just feel inadequate"

Side of Eye: "I'm afraid to make a mistake"

Under Eye: "I need to make sure I don't make a mistake."

Under Nose: "What if they find out I'm not perfect?"

Chin: "I need to be perfect or I'll get in trouble."

Collarbone: "I'm just not good enough."

Under Arm: "What if they find out I'm not good enough?"

Top of Head: "I've never been good enough."

Eyebrow: "I never feel good enough."

Side of Eye: "I feel anxious that I haven't done enough."

Under Eye: "I feel anxious that I'm not perfect."

Under Nose: "I feel anxious all the time."

Chin: "I'm so worried that I'm not enough and never will be."

Collarbone: "I feel anxious that I've made a mistake."

Under Arm: "I never feel I'm good enough."

Tap on these statements until you get the intensity level down to a 2 or lower. You will need go back to the earliest time in your childhood when you experienced those physical sensations. Then tap on that specific childhood issue. Perhaps your parents told you, "You aren't good enough to succeed." Perhaps if your family was addicted or ill, you thought if you behaved better, they would be better. After all, children oftentimes think that if something is wrong in the family, that it is their fault. Perhaps you were compared unfavorably to a sibling who did better than you.

When you get the intensity level low enough, you can use something like the following positive statements.

Karate Chop: "Even though I am not perfect, I am good enough just the way I am and I completely love and accept myself."

OR

"Even though other people might judge or criticize me, I deeply and completely love and accept myself."

OR

(Some other similar statement.)

Top of Head: "I am enough."

Eyebrow: "I am a valuable person even though I am not perfect."

Side of Eye: "I don't need to be perfect anymore."

Under Eye: "It's OK if I make mistakes."

Under Nose: "I am enough even if I'm not perfect."

Chin: "Even if others criticize me, I am good enough."

Collarbone: "It feels so good to know I'm doing enough."

Under Arm: "I am enough and valuable even though I make mistakes."

Chapter 13

Kick Overwhelm to the Curb

So many mothers complain about how they are constantly overwhelmed with things they need to do, but they never seem to accomplish enough. "How can I take on another task?"

The information on these pages can help you overcome overwhelm and get you into your flow and into your go! It is not a miracle cure and it will take practice

EXERCISE: *Time Management Tip*

1. Look at your to-do list and prioritize the tasks by importance:

Most important tasks (A)

Less important tasks (B)

Not necessary to be done today. (C)

2. Look at the most important tasks on your list. Assign a number to each task. Which one is the hardest to do? Or the most important? Perhaps it is the cold calls you need to make each day. You are feeling some reluctance to do that task. How high is your resistance with 10 being the highest and 1 being the lowest resistance? Tap on that issue until the number goes down to a 1 or 2.

3. Do the tapping with each item that seems difficult.

4. Then do the hardest task first.

You'll be amazed that your day will be so much more pleasant. You may also be surprised at how much more you will accomplish. Managing your time in this way will handle a good part of the overwhelm that you might experience. It is also important to realize that if a task is at a C level, and you accomplish the A and some of the B tasks, you do not berate yourself for not finishing the C tasks. Focus on giving yourself credit for what you do accomplish.

Now that you have done these exercises and done some tapping, take a few minutes to review what you have learned about yourself.

Remember to start with only one area of your life that you wish to change or improve. It may be that you're a perfectionist. Perhaps you feel guilty that you aren't Super Mom. Perhaps you get angry with the children too often and not for good reasons. Whatever you choose, just choose one thing to start with. You may find down the road that several items are inter-connected. If you try to work on too many things at once, you won't be as successful as you might wish and you will feel overwhelmed.

Take the projects and put simpler, quicker steps under each project. Writing a book can seem too huge to be able to finish! It is a project and it needs to be broken down into smaller steps. The first step might be to decide on chapter headings. Then I might look at old papers I've written. Next I might arrange these papers into my chapters. I might write one chapter at a time. And so on. As I look at the smaller steps, each step seems manageable. Each day that I do one task, I can check it off and feel like I've accomplished something important. The sense of accomplishment is important to defeat overwhelm. When I have a lot of days when I can't accomplish anything, then there is an emotional component to be handled. Or maybe I'm expect-ing too much of myself and need to look at how big my tasks are.

Tom was a people pleaser. He completely avoided confrontation with any-one including his wife, coworkers, and children. Everyone wanted him to do more and more for them. He felt bad about the things he "should" do, but never had enough time to do them.

Overwhelm can be caused by not knowing what steps to take or by unex-pressed (and often unrealized) emotions. You can only start from where you are. Sometimes you need coaching or counseling to learn the correct steps to take. You need a strategic action plan. If you are not taking action, you need to question if there is an emotional component that's stopping you. Then take small steps one at a time to accomplish your goals. The key is to take action—small steps at a time—not an immediate leap.

Sometimes feeling overwhelmed is a way of the body telling you that you need to handle certain unresolved emotions before you can take action.

Tom had to work on childhood abuse that he witnessed. He then learned how to stand up for himself.

Avoid Noise Pollution and Violence

Choose entertainment (TV and movies) wisely to avoid being triggered by violence. Choose lighter fare instead. Whether you pick up a newspaper or turn on the television, there is a lot of violence. Cell phones are kept visible constantly. Many of the most popular games for adults and children feature violence. Do not watch violence in the movies or on television. Watching violence in movies or TV can trigger the emotional feeling that you experienced in a past trauma. There are a lot of feel good movies and books available for you to choose.

When you are eating, do not discuss topics that are painful to anyone at the table. That means you do not discuss bad grades or discipline of the children. Do not argue about anything at the dinner table. I know that many families don't have dinner time together at a table because so many individuals have different schedules and many people like to watch TV while eating. But there are many rewards to having a pleasant family dinner.

Many people don't think of their homes as "noisy," but a constantly running television can make the overall noise level a threat to concentration and a cause of stress. In fact, children from more noisy homes do suffer ill effects from this type of sound pollution that includes less cognitive growth, delayed language skills, increased anxiety, and impaired resilience according to a Purdue University study.

A noisy office environment, too, can trigger the body's stress response and the high levels of stress hormones that go with it.

EXERCISE: *Tapping Reduces Stress and the Feeling of Overwhelm*
Tapping

(Emotional Freedom Technique) has been proven to lower the stress level in individuals. This is because the cortisol level (as shown in some double bind experiments) goes down as people tap.

Start by giving yourself a score from 0 to 10 with 10 being the most overwhelmed possible and 0 being no overwhelm. Write this number down.

Tap the Karate Chop point 3 times saying out loud:

"Even though I'm stressed out and overwhelmed, I deeply and completely love and accept myself."

"Even though I have too much to do and I feel like I'll never complete it, I deeply and completely love and accept myself."

"There's just too much to do, and I can't get it done, but I deeply and completely love and accept myself."

Tap each of the other points (5 to 7 Times) saying the following statements out loud:

Round 1

Top of Head: "These feelings of overwhelm."

Eyebrow: "All this overwhelm that I can't control."

Side of Eye: "I just can't get all this work done."

Under Eye: "So stressed out about this overwhelm."

Under Nose: "Feeling that I'll never be able to relax."

Chin: "All these feelings of overwhelm."

Collarbone: "There's not enough hours in the day."

Under Arm: "All these feelings of overwhelm."

Round 2

Top of Head: "All these feelings of overwhelm."

Eyebrow: "There's just too much to do."

Side of Eye: "I'll never be able to relax."

Under Eye: "Not enough hours in the day."

Under Nose: "All these feelings of overwhelm."

Chin: "So stressed out about this overwhelm."

Collarbone: "Too much to do."

Under Arm: "Stressed out and overwhelmed."

Round 3 *(When the intensity level is down to less than 3.)*

Top of Head: "Maybe I can give myself permission to relax."

Eyebrow: "A lot to do, but being stressed out doesn't help."

Side of Eye: "Maybe I can praise myself every time I accomplish a little task."

Under Eye: "Let go of some of these feelings of overwhelm."

Under Nose: "Breathe out these feelings of overwhelm."

Chin: "Give myself permission to relax."

Collarbone: "I have the ability to do what has to be done."

Under Arm: "I choose to let go of the feeling of being overwhelmed."

Take a deep breath.

Now scan your feelings and again score the feeling of overwhelm on a scale of 0 to 10. Most people find that the number has gone down.

You can repeat this sequence several times sequentially and several times a day. It is important to always write down the numbers because when the numbers go down, sometimes is hard to believe that the numbers were higher at the beginning.

Chapter 14

Embrace Powerful Empowering Beliefs

If we know what we want and we know how to get it, but still don't succeed in getting it, then perhaps there's an emotional component stopping us. Different guides have called it by different names. I use the term limiting beliefs. **Everyone agrees that our beliefs about how worthy we feel, or what we deserve, or what we can accomplish are the real reasons that so many people fail at what they are trying to achieve.** Making it even worse, we often pass these limiting beliefs down to our children—generation after generation.

Limiting beliefs are the beliefs that are unconscious, semi-conscious, or fully conscious that you may have about how the world is. Unfortunately, these beliefs are not true, but we believe and act as if they are true. For example, I had the belief that the world is not a safe place for me to let the world know who I am. Now it may be true, that it was not safe for me to tell a lot of people about my parents. But I generalized and kept a lot of information to myself. This hurt me in my relationships with people both personal and at work.

It's time to get past those old issues of worth. It's time to believe with all your heart and soul that you really do deserve your abundance! You really do deserve to have less stress and more peace of mind. You really do deserve to have a happy family.

EXERCISE:

In an earlier chapter, we discussed being clear about what's stopping you from achieving that goal? If you look at one goal that has been eluding you for some time, but you really want to achieve it, you might try saying the following three statements out loud—with conviction. Say them while you're looking in a mirror or talking to a friend.

"It's possible!"

"I can do it!"

"I deserve it!"

Some people find it difficult to say all three statements with conviction. There is a nagging voice within that seems to answer back, "NO!"

We soak up opinions from our parents. Some parents give their children a piece of candy for a reward. These individuals can grow up believing that food is a reward if they do something good—or a consolation prize if they have a problem. The children continue the pattern of snacking and start hating the scale.

Other parents downgrade an education, saying within earshot of a child, "He thinks he's a real smart ass just because he has a degree." The adult might wonder why she isn't motivated to go to college.

Perhaps, while growing up, a woman heard: "Money is the root of all evil." "You can't be spiritual and have a lot of money." "Money doesn't grow on trees." She might wonder why she is always struggling to get money.

One way to conquer this is to **write and say** affirmations. The affirmation should assume that your goal is possible and achievable. It should be stated in a positive statement.

"I am going to weigh _____ pounds."
"I am feeling better and better about myself."
"By this time next year I will be earning $_____."
"I will be in a great relationship within 2 years."
"I can handle conflicts with other people in a very reasonable manner."

Say your affirmations out loud several times a day. Focus your mind on them by having them written where you can see them often. You can pay attention to the feelings inside your body as you say these statements out loud. It is difficult or easy to believe these statements.

Pay attention to the conversations that you have with other people. How do you talk and think about motherhood, money, weight, or relationships? How did your parents feel about parenting, money, weight, or relationships, etc.? Did you soak up their beliefs?

Are there negative phrases such as, "Not really," or "Yeah, right," that you keep repeating to yourself whenever you think of your abundance goals? Some people may be able to discover their limiting beliefs by listening to their own internal conversations. You might listen to the times you sell yourself short or tell other people you can't do something.

One very good reason to examine what your beliefs are is to think of what you want your children to accomplish. If you believe that having a comfortable life style is unattainable, you may be conditioning your children to believe that. (Although it is possible that your child may decide to be completely different from you and make a lot of money.)

If you think that confrontations with other people are bad, and you avoid conflict at any cost you might be surprised to find out how your adult child is taken advantage of by his or her spouse.

These limiting beliefs trip people up when they try to achieve their goals. You need to be clear about any limiting beliefs that you might have. Then you need to change them into empowering beliefs that allow you to achieve your goals. Then you will know that it is possible to achieve them and you deserve to achieve them. This shift in mindset allows you to see the path and then motivates you to continue the journey to your abundance. It brings a greater joy to the children in that they are freer to pursue their dreams.

Here are some limiting beliefs that others have had about their goals. Do any of these sound familiar?

"I'm afraid to become too successful (have money, a nice figure, good job, great relationship, etc.)"

"I keep sabotaging myself."

"I find myself feeling guilty because I have more than others."

"I'm afraid of becoming wealthy because of other people's reactions."

"I see wealthy people as greedy, lucky, mean, or unfair."

"I feel guilty because I want more."

"I'm afraid they'll reject me if I become successful."

"I'm afraid I might reject them if I get what I want."

"I'm afraid they will envy me."

"I don't want to stand out."

"I'm afraid I won't fit in again."

"I'm afraid they'll think I'm greedy if I'm rich."

"I don't want them to be jealous of me."

"I feel 'less than' around people with (money, a nice figure, good job, etc.)."

"I don't believe I can make more money (get a good job, have a good figure, have a great relationship, etc.)."

"If I have more, I'll be taking away from others."

"There will always be shortages."

Empowering Beliefs: A Magical Key to the Abundance You Deserve

Sally noticed that whenever she talked about money, she always said she had enough. Yet, she wondered why she didn't have extra money for splurging on vacations or restaurants. Then one day in a group setting where they focused on money beliefs (the exercise is included in this chapter), she realized that "having enough, **but no more**" was her limiting belief. Without realizing it, she had repeatedly stated that she always felt she could enjoy enough money. She knew she thought about money this way, but she never connected the dots to realize that that was why she didn't earn **more** money.

Although she was a school teacher with a fixed salary, she had a condo that she used to live in before her second marriage. With her second husband, she had bought a condo that she was living in. She decided that after the mortgage was paid off, she would be able to rent it out and get perhaps $1,000 a month rent to help her retirement. A friend suggested selling that condo and buying apartment units. Initially she laughed at the idea, but then she took a deep breath and sold the condo. She looked for months for an apartment unit and finally found what she wanted. Within a year, she was earning more than the $1,000 a month—and she wasn't retired yet. Another apartment building was to follow that one. After this realization, she transformed that belief and started enjoying a large flow of money in her life.

Exercise: Belief Statements for Goals

Let's discover if you have any limiting beliefs about your goals. If possible do this next exercise with a partner or friend. The idea is to have your partner read the statement and where there's a blank you say the very first thing that comes to mind (**no editing allowed**!). With the belief statements about goals, your partner can say, "People who have (money, relationship, etc.— whatever you want to work on) are _____." You fill in the word. Your partner writes down your response. You may be surprised at what comes to mind, but this will usually give you something concrete to work on.

Remember, choose only one of these at a time for future tapping.

People who have _____ are _____.

Getting _____ makes people _____.

My mother thought that people who had _____ were _____.

My dad thought people who had _____ were _____.

Getting _____ will cause _____.

_____ equals _____.

If I had (or were) _____ I'd _____.

If I could have _____ forever, I'd _____.

I'm afraid that if I was _____, I'd _____.

_____ is _____.

_____ causes _____.

Having _____ is not _____.

When I have _____, I usually _____.

In order to have _____, I'd need to _____.

The scary part about having _____is _____.

People think _____ is _____.

Not having _____, tells me _____.

Having _____ will cause _____.

I think people who have _____ are _____.

My friends think that people who have _____ are _____.

Weight Beliefs

Thinner people are _____.

Getting thinner makes people _____.

I'd stay thin if _____.

My parents thought thinner people were _____.

Getting thinner will cause _____.

Overweight equals _____.

If I were thin I'd _____.

If I could stay thin forever, I'd _____.

I'm afraid that if I was thin, I'd _____.

Thin is _____.

Being overweight is _____.

In order to stay thin, I'd need to _____.

The scary part about being thin is _____.

In order to get thin I'd need to _____.

When I am thin, I usually _____.

If I weren't so overweight, I'd _____.

People think being thin is _____.

People think being overweight is _____.

Being overweight tells me _____.

I think people who are thin are _____.

Money Beliefs

People with money are _____.

Money makes people _____.

I'd have more money if _____.

My dad thought money was _____.

My mom always thought money would _____.

In my family, money caused _____.

Money equals _____.

If I had money I'd _____.

If I could afford it, I'd _____.

If I had some money, I'd _____.

I'm afraid that if I had money I would _____.

Money is _____.

Money causes _____.

Having money is not _____.

In order to have more money, I'd need to _____.

When I have money, I usually _____.

I think money _____.

If I weren't so cheap, I'd _____.

People think money _____.

Being broke tells me _____.

Relationship Beliefs

People with good relationships are _____.

Relationships make people _____.

I'd have a relationship if _____.

My dad thought relationships were _____.

My mom always thought relationships would _____.

In my family the relationships were _____.

If I had a relationship, I'd_____.

If I had a good relationship, I'd _____.

I'm afraid if I had a good relationship, I'd _____.

A good relationship is _____.

Relationships cause _____.

Having a relationship is not _____.

When I have a relationship, I usually _____.

In order to have a good relationship, I'd need to _____.

People think a good relationship _____.

Not having a good relationship tells me _____.

Having a good relationship will cause _____.

EXERCISE: EFT to conquer limiting beliefs

Karate Chop (or sore spot): (Set-up statement) "Even though I feel I don't deserve to have _____(my goal) I deeply and completely love and accept myself."

"Even though it's not possible for me to have my goal, I deeply and completely love and accept myself."

"Even though I don't feel that I can succeed, I deeply and completely love and accept myself."

Eyebrow: "I don't deserve to have what I want."

Side of Eye: "I feel so anxious about achieving my goal."

Under Eye: "I feel scared to reach my goal."

Under Nose: "It's impossible for me to reach my goal."

Chin: "I will be alone if I reach my goal."

Collarbone: "I am very stressed out right now."

Under Arm: "They'll be jealous of me if I succeed."

Top of Head: "I feel guilty because I want more."

Now for positive focus on the problem.

Gamut Point: "It is possible to achieve my goal and I deserve to have my goal."

Eyebrow: "I choose to feel peaceful about achieving my goal."

Side of Eye: "It is possible for me to succeed."

Under Eye: "My friends will be happy if I succeed."

Under Nose: "I appreciate how relaxed I can feel even though I have this problem."

Chin: "It's OK to be scared and nervous about a change."

Collarbone: "Thank you, universe, for the creative guidance."

Under Arm: "I deserve to reach my goal."

Top of Head: "I enjoy the challenge of becoming successful in reaching my goal."

Tap on following phrases as you complete one more round.

"I love knowing we all deserve abundance."

"I choose to believe in the guidance I am receiving."

"I appreciate the prosperity in my life."

"I love appreciating my body, my friends, my opportunities."

"I'm grateful for all the new opportunities for abundance."

"I appreciate exactly who I am."

"I appreciate all the lessons I have learned."

"I am so grateful for all the prosperity in my life."

Getting More Specific About Eliminating the Limiting Beliefs.

As you think about any of these limiting beliefs that are very strong in your life, you will need to tune into the physical sensation that you are experiencing. Get as specific as you can. Remember the first time in your life that you experienced that feeling. Go to the event, give it a name and then telling yourself the story as you tap. Remember to halt the story whenever you are going to start a section with a big emotional charge. Number the physical sensation and the emotional feeling with the intensity level. (1 —10) Tap until you lower the intensity level to less than a 3. Then continue the story.

You may need to tap on several instances of this physical and emotional sensation. If the intensity level is too high to begin with, you need to tap with an experienced practitioner.

As long as you have limiting beliefs, you will not be able to achieve your goals. To get some more scripts to help you eliminate these limiting beliefs, go to my website and get free audios with some more limiting beliefs tapping scripts.

You'll also receive the special bonus I created to make it easier to do the tapping exercises that are an integral part of this book. I have recorded six "tap along" MP3s to help you become an expert tapper. When you finish this book, you will be armed with the skills to effectively handle many of the challenges that you face as a working Mother.

Go to http://www.sheilahenry.com/Bonus.en.html to register for your gift. As another bonus you will also receive tips and information on stress from time to time. You may of course unsubscribe at any time.

The sooner you know how to manage stress, the sooner you'll feel in control.

Chapter 15

Gain Victory Over Guilt, Anger, and Shame

When you feel guilty about something you said or did, or perhaps didn't do, or you feel ashamed about something, then you don't feel you deserve success. These feelings can be much more powerful than any positive affirmations—and thus stop affirmations from manifesting.

One of the biggest causes career mothers feel guilty is that they don't spend enough time with their children or their spouse. They're too tired some nights to read a bedtime story to their child. Dinner was too late and wasn't the most nutritious meal. On top of that, everyone else in the office stayed later to work on a project. Daycare hours are strict about closing times so they left early.

Some mothers feel guilty for not being an at-home mother. Or perhaps the problem is the combination of work with being a mother. There are many problems.

When the child is still a baby, childcare is extremely expensive and some women learn that by the time they pay for childcare, transportation, and work clothes, there is no money left from their earnings. Oftentimes there is no skilled childcare available. If there are no relatives who will assume the burden of day care, then the mother must stay home. We won't even talk about being tired from a full-time job and then trying to be a good mother at night. Although some mothers try to work at home, that is only an option for a few mothers.

When the child or children are old enough to go to school, there is still a problem with school hours. School hours are much shorter than work hours. Some women are lucky enough to get part-time jobs or sales jobs that pay commission only. For other women who have had jobs in fast food restaurants, there has been a problem (partially ameliorated) with restaurants constantly shifting work hours and giving last minute notice to mothers.

This has played havoc with women being able to schedule reliable care for their children.

Some single mothers are forced to work since that income is their only income. Married women may choose to be at-home mothers for several years. They may or may not have the support of their partner. Or their partner may be emotionally supportive, but they need the money for food and rent.

Or a partner may be resentful that he needs to earn the money and she "gets to stay home" all day. (Many men may not realize all the work involved in child care, cleaning and cooking.) Some women who are stay at home moms become bored with just the interaction with children. They crave the intercourse with other adults.

When children want to participate in school or community activities, it often involves a parent driving them places. If parents have a job, they might have to leave at 2:30 p.m. to pick up a child and chauffeur them someplace. If a mother is responsible, it oftentimes means she has a sales job or a part-time job (with lower pay).

Perhaps a big part of the guilt is the expectation that some women have that they can be Super Moms. They expect themselves to do it all and have it all. What to do? They have read that they can have it all, but the reality is different from fantasy. It is extremely difficult to have a work/home life balance. Perhaps women CAN have it all, but not at the same time.

It is very important to have choices and to know that you have choices. I am going to get very political here because political choices do affect our private lives. Don't have a child until you are ready. That means that all children should be educated in sexuality (including contraceptives) in school. Education has helped teenage girls from having unwanted pregnancies. Where education and contraceptives are available, abortion rates have gone way down.

It is much easier to raise a child with two parents, rather than one. Although if a single man or woman wants to have a child, there should be a way for adoptions or other ways to have this child.

It is so important for women to have the right to make their own reproductive choices. If a woman gets pregnant accidentally, if she is raped, or if she finds out that the fetus is gravely impaired, she should not have her whole life shattered. If this is not the right time to have a child, or she realizes that the man who got her pregnant is not a good partner, then she should be able to chart the course of her own life and make her medical decisions about her body with her doctor.

When a couple wants to have a child, there should be discussion about the time and emotional commitment needed. How will they finance this child? Will the mother (or father) work part time or will one of them stay home for several years? Although they may agree on a course of action, life may get in the way. My decision was to work and it didn't occur to me to be a stay at home mom. But I had to take a leave of absence for six months, because of my son's illness.

Know you are making a choice. Perhaps, if you're lucky, you are making many of the decisions. Step #1 is to take responsibility for your choices. Children take a lot of time and energy. When they get sick, you lose sleep. A parent cannot do and be everything for everybody.

Step #2 is to get rid of any guilt you may have about not being either a perfect mother or a perfect career woman. I find that one of the greatest reasons for feeling guilty is the feeling that you are failing because of a balance between work and family. If you choose to work, you need to get over any guilt you may have about not spending enough time with your children, or not having the energy to have a perfectly clean home. You may not have the ability to stay overtime at the job and compete with some of the single people. There are just so many hours in the day and just so much energy that you have. If you choose to stay at home, you may have to give up feeling guilty about not helping enough with the finances.

All these guilt feelings may make you want to punish yourself. One of the reasons that people feel they are sabotaging themselves and not getting what they want in life is this need to punish themselves. If you discover any of these feelings within yourself, it is necessary to be able to accept and then forgive yourself. You are releasing an energy that is holding you back.

EXERCISE: *Tapping Script for Guilt*

Please realize that these are only suggestions to get you started. Substitute your own words where possible. You want to give an intensity rating from 1 to 10 on how strong your feeling of guilt is. You also want to pay attention to any sensations in your body.

In order to tap away these feelings, you need to be in touch with them. Sometimes people have "stuffed" their feelings for many years or decades. This makes it difficult to unearth the feelings of guilt.

Karate Chop: "Even though I feel guilty because I am (*insert your situation*), I deeply & completely love and accept myself." *(Repeat 3 times.)*

Top of Head: "I feel so guilty."

Eyebrow: "I am just stuck and I don't know what to do."

Side of Eye: "I should be able to do *(insert your situation)*."

Under Eye: "I should be a perfect mother."

Under Nose: "I'm not a good enough mother."

Chin: "I'm not doing a good job at work."

Collarbone: "I'm always tired and overwhelmed."

Under Arm: "My children are deprived and suffering."

Top of Head: "Why can't I do better?"

Eyebrow: "I'm just not good enough."

Side of Eye: "I feel so guilty about not being a good mother."

Under Eye: "I just want to run away and hide."

Under Nose: "I never imagined it would be so hard."

Chin: "I'm not a good wife either. I never have time with my husband."

Collarbone: "Why is it so hard?"

Under Arm: "I just feel so guilty."

When your intensity rating has gone down to a 2 or less, you may want to do a round of affirmative tapping.

Top of Head: "I am doing the best job that I can."

Eyebrow: "I don't have to be Super Mom because there's no such thing."

Side of Eye: "I am learning to compliment myself for my hard work."

Under Eye: "I can spend time enjoying my children."

Under Nose: "I give myself credit for taking on this difficult job."

Chin: "I put my energy into sharing love with my children and spouse."

Collarbone: "Our family communicates fully and openly and with love."

Under Arm: "I can relax with the knowledge that I am doing my best."

Check your intensity level.

Anger

Another oftentimes buried feeling is anger. Sometimes a person might feel guilty because of anger against a handicapped relative. Maybe some people feel anger towards a parent that abused them emotionally or physically. I have had adults come in and tell me that they have "forgiven" their parent, but it is obvious that this is only an intellectual exercise. Perhaps you are angry with your parents because you were never allowed to say "No."

Do you feel angry with someone or some people in your life and you do not express it to them?

You have been told that it is wrong to feel anger and so you bury the feeling. But it comes out in the way that you treat other people. It is also true that people who suffer from chronic pain will often feel some relief when they are able to let go of the anger. Perhaps it's expressed in never saying "No!" to your boss, friends or spouse. Whether there is unexpressed anger or too much anger, anger is a problem.

Are you still furious about some incident in your past that you think may, or may not, have been resolved? Some people often have excessive anger after a small event. If this happens, it is quite likely anger has been triggered by some past experiences.

Sometimes we feel anger towards others because we believe they should have done something that they didn't do… or didn't do something you thought they should have done. The key thought here is **should.** Should has been considered the dirtiest word in the English language. There's a wonderful expression that I have often heard and repeated to my clients: **"Don't should on yourself!"**

If you do have chronic anger problems, it is a good idea to get some help from a professional counselor who has been trained on how to manage anger issues.

EXERCISE: Tapping Script for Anger

Karate Chop: "Even though I am so angry at _____ because he/she did _____, I deeply and completely love and accept myself."

OR

"Even though I am so angry with my boss because he/she _____, I deeply and completely love and accept myself."

OR

"Even though I am so angry with my parents because they loved my brother more than me, I deeply and completely love and accept myself."

Top of Head: "I'm so angry at _____."

Eyebrow: (*Answering the question, Why?*) "I'm angry because he/she _____."

Side of Eye: (*Where do you feel it in your body?*) "I feel this anger in my _____. It feels like _____."

Under Eye: "He/she should/shouldn't have done _____."

Under Nose: "I'm just so angry."

Chin: "I don't know if I'll ever trust him/her again."

Collarbone: "This has really fouled me up."

Under Arm: "I'm so very angry."

As you tap several rounds you might ask yourself, "Does this make me recall an earlier incident in my childhood when I was angry and felt these same sensations in my body?" Then tap on that earlier incident.

Shame

Shame is another one of the inner negative voices that get in your way of achieving your goals. It manifests itself in beliefs such as: "The truth is I'm not good enough." "I really don't deserve more." "There must be something wrong with me." "I'll never fit in!"

Perhaps there is something that you could have done, you feel you should have done, and you didn't. Or you did something that you shouldn't have done. Maybe others know of your misdeeds. How do you live this down? How do you face others who may know of your misdeeds? How do you face yourself and let go of the shame?

Some people might hang on to the shame hoping to tell themselves not to make the same mistake again. Secretly, they are afraid that they will make the same mistake again. They won't let go.

Some people feel shame about their body. Perhaps they are overweight and go on diet after diet and then regain the weight (plus additional pounds). Perhaps they have some physical handicap such as walking with a limp from childhood polio, or facial acne, or poor eyesight or anything in their body which they think sets them apart from the norm. Race is another area that some people suffer from.

What messages and attitudes of shame did you get from your parents, siblings, teachers, or babysitters? Is there something that you did (or didn't do) that has made you ashamed?

EXERCISE: *Belief Statements About Guilt, Anger & Shame*

I should have done _____.

If only I had _____.

I shouldn't have done _____.

He/she should have done _____

I'm so ashamed of _____

If they knew I had done _____, they would _____.

I can't let anyone know I did _____.

I don't deserve to _____.

For someone who has carried around a trauma, fear, anger, grief or guilt or other issue for many years the emotion becomes part of their identity. Perhaps it's something you want to accomplish and just can't seem to get there. Or perhaps it's consistently doing something you don't want to do such as smoking, drinking, eating, or gambling.

Although consciously people want to get rid of their problem oftentimes their subconscious (the emotional part of the brain) holds on to it. Overcoming or losing that "identity" can be very threatening to the non-rational part of the brain.

EXERCISE:

The first step would be to understand the underlying benefit of holding on to the issue. Most people say that there is no benefit. But there always is. The following questions could help you realize what the benefit is.

If I get rid of this _____, then _____ would happen.

People will no longer give me sympathy _____.

I'll have to _____ if I change.

It's not safe to change because _____.

They won't pay attention to me anymore.

I'm afraid if I let this go that _____.

I won't know myself.

What if I succeed and my life still sucks?

What if I still can't get (a promotion, new friends, a lover, better relationships)?

I'll lose my friends.

I don't deserve to have what I want.

I won't know how to act if I succeed.

When you know what some of these issues are, then when you do some tapping, you will use the Karate Chop point to reverse them.

"Even though I have *(problem)*, **and I don't want to overcome it,** I deeply and completely love and accept myself."

Chapter 16

Transform Your Inner Critic to a Powerful Ally

Tania came into my office telling me that she wanted to change jobs and get into a company where she was appreciated and she had better secretarial help. Every time she thought of applying for a job, she would first say to herself, "Yes, I would be perfect for this job." Then she would reflect and it seemed like there was a part inside of her that said, "No, you're not good enough for this job. They'd never hire you." She didn't know why she would think things like that. But it happened over and over. We identified and labeled this Inner Critical Voice that stopped her from even trying to get a job. I helped her understand that this voice had been with her since childhood. I showed her how to transform this inner critic to a powerful ally. She was then able to apply for and get a much better job.

Do you have an inner voice that seems to control you by saying things such as the following?

"You can't succeed."
"You're not good enough."
"You don't deserve that."

Every time you think that you will do something or have something, then we need to transform this Inner Critical Voice into a voice that can help you succeed.

EXERCISE: *Communicating with your Inner Voice or Critic*

For this you need to sit in a quiet place, close your eyes and have the following conversation with this voice.

Ask the voice if it will communicate with you. When the voice says, "Yes," then thank the voice and you can then can ask the next question: "How are you trying to help me?"

Many people protest over the second question. But the reality is that this voice is trying to help. Most of the time, **the voice is trying to protect you,** but ends up hindering you. It may take some tapping or repeated efforts before the voice will tell you how it is protecting you. When you get an answer, or a partial answer, thank the voice.

Ask the voice, "Would you be open to find some other way to help or protect me since the way that you are doing is actually hurting me?" If the voice says, "No," then thank it and try going through these steps another day. If the voice says, "Yes!" then thank it and ask it to come up with some other ways. Or you might think of other ways to suggest to the voice how it might help.

As you or the voice thinks of other ways to help with the protection, ask the voice, "Would you be willing to try this new way?" The voice might say, "Yes" or "No," to any of the ways. Either way, thank the voice for its help. You may have at least one new way for the voice to help.

The voice might direct you to a past incident that needs to be tapped on. This is because so many of the decisions that we make are from childhood when we made decisions with the best knowledge we had at the time. However, as adults we do not have to be bound by childhood decisions that no longer serve us well.

What I have personally learned from talking to my Inner Critic about not feeling that this is a safe world is that it wanted to protect me. But I told it that the way it was protecting me was harming me. My Inner Critic agreed to protect me in a different way. It would help me vet who I could reveal myself to and when to keep quiet. This is a much better way of protecting me and it has led to much better relationships in my life.

The other way we are transforming the Inner Critic to an empowering helper is by tapping. You will notice that we start the tapping by stating the problem that we are experiencing. We state the physical sensation. By then going to the earliest time when we experienced that physical sensation, we get to the root cause of that Inner Critic. We defuse the decision that we made when we were children or in a more vulnerable position. We pay attention to the various sensory elements: Sight, sound, emotion, and, possibly, taste and smell. We then go on to tap in the positive suggestions.

Oftentimes during the tapping about the young age, we have an "aha" moment. "Oh, this is why I do or say _____." That can be enough for us to make the necessary change. There are times when you have this aha moment that you laugh at how funny your earlier decisions were. The laughter is great. It shows that this outdated decision or belief is of no more consequence.

Since parents pass down these limiting beliefs to their children—sometimes even for generation after generation—you are breaking a negative cycle. By eliminating these limiting beliefs, you are giving your children greater opportunity for a fulfilling life.

PART IV

HARNESS YOUR INNER STRENGTHS AND ASSETS

Chapter 17

Expand Your Circle of Comfort

We have a resistance to change. Sometimes the situation is so stressful, but at least we know what to expect if we remain the same. This is called our "circle of comfort." Change can be scary because it's like jumping off a cliff. We don't know what to expect if we change the way we do things. We "protect" ourselves by not changing and handling the unresolved issues and feelings that we have.

You *must move your circle of comfort* to better levels and you must address the specific impediments to performance that need improvement.

EXERCISE: *Tapping to Expand Your Circle of Comfort*

For tapping, the set-up phrase you use must include the new level of performance. Examples:

"Even though I still have a lot of tension at my job, and am not completely at ease, I deeply and completely love and accept myself.

"Even though I just don't feel attractive enough, I deeply and completely love and accept myself.

"Even though I am not yet earning $100,000 a year, I deeply and completely love and accept myself.

"Even though I'm still too tired to spend several hours a day with my children, I deeply and completely love and accept myself.

"Even though I'm afraid to change, I deeply and completely love and accept myself.

"Even though they won't like me if I change, I deeply and completely love and accept myself."

"Even though success can be very scary, I deeply and completely love and accept myself."

"Even though this is all anybody expects of me, I deeply and completely love and accept myself."

"Even though I don't want to rock the boat, I deeply and completely love and accept myself."

"Even though I don't know how to handle success, I deeply and completely love and accept myself."

"Even though all my friends also have this problem, I deeply and completely love and accept myself."

"Even though it's easier to stay where I am, I deeply and completely love and accept myself."

"Even though it's too hard to try to achieve my goal, I deeply and completely love and accept myself."

"Even though it's hard for me to imagine _____, I deeply and completely love and accept myself."

"Even though I haven't gotten close to believing _____, I deeply and completely love and accept myself."

"Even though I have trouble thinking of myself _____, I deeply and completely love and accept myself."

After the set-up phrase, you need to look at **specific past events** where you got the idea that you couldn't achieve what you wanted. Go back to looking at your list of limiting beliefs you created earlier.

EXERCISE: *Expand Your Circle of Comfort*

Stand in a room and draw an imaginary circle in front of you. This is a big circle which can expand as you do this exercise. The exercise involves placing different items in the circle:

Friends
Your favorite piece of music
A pet you love
Your favorite books

Your favorite vacation places
Loved family members
Hobbies you love
Your favorite colors
Favorite places to meditate or just be you
Possessions you love
Anything else you care about

Probably your imaginary circle has gotten bigger. Close your eyes. Notice how you feel as you are outside the circle. What's happening with your body? What's happening with your emotions?

Now with your eyes still closed, step inside the circle. Notice your body and your emotions.

Now step out of the circle and again notice your body and emotions.

Go inside the circle or stay outside—whichever feels better. Then open your eyes. Know that you can take this imaginary circle with you wherever you go. **It is now your circle of comfort.**

Most people who do this exercise feel stronger and better about themselves afterwards.

Chapter 18

Envision Your Strengths

There is a belief that it is better to spend most of the time that we work on ourselves working on our problems and weaknesses. However, experts who have studied happiness and well-being suggest that it is much more helpful to work on improving the areas where you are already strong.

Some of us may have difficulty recognizing our strengths. I took the Signature Strengths exam and found out that one of my personal strengths was forgiveness. This surprised me. But as I thought about it, I realized that I have never been a person to hold grudges. I didn't understand why people would hold grudges. I also resisted teaching about forgiveness. I did it so automatically, that I didn't even realize how I did it. I had to really study the process of forgiveness so that I could teach others how to use it. A lot of us are so good at something that we don't realize how we do it or even think about it as a skill to use.

I invite you to take Martin Seligman's Signature Strength Test to learn more about yourself.

EXERCISE: *Signature Strengths*

To start go to "Martin Seligman Signature Strengths" on your computer and take the free 15-minute VIA Signature Strength exam. Optional: You may wish to buy the longer explanation.

People have wondered whether life would be better if they worked on their weak points or strengthened their existing strengths. People are often much more successful if they emphasize their strengths. (You can also eliminate some of your weaknesses, but this is not where you should concentrate most of your energy—unless you have a really glaring weakness like an addiction or violence.)

I can utilize my strengths more effectively if I _____

EXERCISE: *Recognizing your strengths*

Here is another way that you can learn about your strengths. Ask yourself:

What are some of the things from your past about which you are most proud?

What energizes you in the present?

What are you looking forward to in the near future?

Weaknesses are an important focus. What are some of yours?

What are some of your strengths that are least developed? How could you work on them?

Are there times you use your strongest strengths too much?

EXERCISE: *Creating an Ideal Self*

Describe where you would be living.

What is it you value in living arrangements and circumstances that you would like to achieve?

To what extent is this vision of your future living arrangements internal vs the product of some external factor or someone else's values?

 Describe your work life: your commute, your office, your position, the type of work you would do.

What is it you value in work that you would like to achieve in this ideal future?

To what extent is this vision of your future work the product of internal vs the product of some external factor or someone else's values?

What resources and opportunities do you have that will help you work toward your ideal self?

What hurdles do you anticipate?

Name a single, small behavior you can change as a first step toward your ideal self.

How can you chart your progress toward your ideal self?

As you answer each question, note if there are any emotional reactions to any answer that you may give. You may need to tap on any answer that gives you a feeling of discomfort or stress. Remember as you are tapping to start with the emotional issue and the part of your body where you experience any discomfort.

PART V

NAVIGATE THE DANCE BETWEEN
WORK AND PERSONAL LIFE

Chapter 19

Fight the I Feel-Like-A-Failure Trap

Sally is working a few hours a day and has three children, ages 1 ½, 3, and 10. She would love to stay at home with her kids. Her biggest problem is that she can't even take a breath. When she wants to take a bathroom break, the two youngest pound on the door wondering where their mother is. Although her husband would like to help, he only helps with some housekeeping chores. She's considering whether she would like to home school her children because she just loves being a mother. But would she ever get out with other adults? Would she ever have a minute to herself?

If you are a working mother, you are engaged in an impossible task that needs to be made possible. Many have done it, but there are many sacrifices that have been made. Our society demands impossible choices from parents—and pretends otherwise. In our country parents receive very little time off to care for young children. Public school doesn't start until age 5. Most employers do not allow for career advancement if a mother works part time. If a child is sick, many companies do not allow the parent paid time off or the ability to use her own sick leave. All of this is more difficult in the USA than in many other advanced countries. The moms who take off to care for their children often have a hard time getting back in the career world.

That doesn't mean it can't be done. It means that there are hard choices to make and you should not be discouraged and feel guilty about your difficulties. If you're working, you may not be able to also bake cookies, become active in the PTA, or be a Scout leader. You may not be able to do your fair share in a carpool to take the children to school or to a game. (I personally was helped quite a bit when four other mothers who weren't working took my son to nursery school every day.)

I was lucky. When I was a single mother with a very young child (and no child support), I was a school teacher. I had shorter work hours. If Greg got sick, I could use my own generous sick leave to stay at home with him. But I remember the many times I had to frantically search for caregivers for an hour or two after school. My parents lived in Florida and I was in California. They weren't available for babysitting.

There is a reason that dogs are dubbed man's best friend. They are loyal to the pack (or family), dependable, affectionate, help protect the household (by barking or growling), never say an unkind word, and they provide a lot of fun. They are the best companion for people wanting a walking or running partner. They never say "NO" to an outdoor excursion. Like us, they are also hardwired for social connection. They have helped me keep my sanity at times when I programmed myself for too many activities. A side benefit of dogs is that dog owners sometimes live longer than others.

My dog, Pepper was a big help with my son, Greg. Because I got divorced when Greg was 2 years old, I never had a second child. However, Pepper was an "older sister" and mentor for Greg. When Greg was young and still in a stroller, I would walk with the stroller and Pepper was on my right side. Pepper always wanted to have something in her mouth. She would find a stick or something on the ground and carry it. Greg had to also have a stick to carry. One day there was a huge fight when there was only one stick and they both wanted it. (No one got hurt in this fight.) I finally had to throw the stick away. This story has been a great source of laughter for many years.

Social support or people connection is the greatest predictor of happiness than any other factor: GPA, family income, age, gender, or race. There are many scientific studies that support that finding. Research shows that social support has as much effect on life expectancy as smoking, high blood pressure, obesity, and regular physical activity. Social bonds aren't just predictive of overall happiness, but also of **eventual career achievement, occupational success, and income.**

Social support can be important in your personal life and at work. Bob and I have been together over 25 years. Initially, we found it impossible to work together. We were both losing our temper quite often because we couldn't agree on our goals. When we started looking at real estate investments, we found that we could use our different strengths to create a mind link, or synergy, to forge together a great success. We put out our energy and then things started to happen such as finding the investments that we did. We made mistakes, but in the long run we did very well.

Sometimes you can have business partners and at other times you need to be a single entrepreneur with the help of various individuals at different junctures.

Five years ago my best friend and I decided to start a social group of women who would share with each other the good and bad details of their lives, while supporting each other in what each was attempting to do. We were looking to meet some new people, as well as including some of our friends. We started talking to some dog walkers in the area and then asked them to join us. We have now been meeting twice a month for five years, but we also have a lot of parties and we are currently planning our fourth retreat together. When I shared with the group that I was learning to make films on my computer, one of the women who had worked in Hollywood offered to go over production values with me. I am taking her up on her offer and I am quite excited by the support of my friends.

Another very important source of support for me has been my Rotary membership. I believe that many service clubs and other organizations help you meet people who are there both with advice or other business connections. As you get to know these individuals through meetings, service projects, and social events, you get to know whom to trust. It is delightful to work with the same people over many years.

EXERCISE: *Support systems*

Who are three of your closest friends?

How do they support you and make you happy?

Do you have friends or acquaintances who are not supportive, and you feel like they drain your energy? Who are they? Why are they in your life?

Let's look at your workplace. How strong is your social support there?

What kind of simple things can you do to improve your people connection in your place of business, neighbors, and other mothers?

What kind of things can you do to improve your personal relationships?

One of the saddest things I have seen is when single women give up their personal women friends when they get into a relationship.

Differences between men and women

There are some important differences between men and women. It is important for women to understand these both at home and at work.

Men do not ask as many questions as women do. This is because there is a basic gender difference in the way that men and women perceive questions. Women ask more questions as a way of giving the appearance of equality. Men are more comfortable in the role of giving help or information, but not receiving it, as they do not wish to be put in the "one down" position.

Men and women grow up with different socialization patterns. Boys, as they are growing up, play competitively and learn that there is a hierarchy of command. They position other boys as "one up" or "one down" from them. By asking a question, they feel that they are putting the other person in a "one up" position. Most men will not ask for directions. My aunt (whose nose was like a compass) used to be quite frustrated with my uncle who had no sense of direction. But when they took their children on weekly outings, my uncle drove the car. Invariably he got lost, took the wrong road, and would not listen to my aunt or ask anyone else for directions. He's not unusual that way. Although today we have GPS's to help, the basic idea is still true about asking questions.

Girls, as they grow up, are taught to cooperate or give the appearance of equality in their play with games and conversation. They *suggest* activities or changes to each other. The center of the social life is the "best friend." In the past, they have not played in as many competitive sports and have been accused of not being "team players." (This is the reason so many people have advocated more female competitive sports to be on an equal basis with male sports.) It's all right for a woman to ask questions, because women are on more of an equal footing with each other. Women ask more questions than men.

When women confide in women, they enjoy being questioned about their feelings. They share similar experiences and feelings. Often, when women confide a problem to a man, she is chagrined that he responds to the confidence as a question. He proposes a solution. This sends the message to the woman that, "She has the problems and he has the answers." Or, instead of asking probing questions, he will change the subject. Women may get angry not realizing that he is respecting her need for independence.

Iris complained that her husband didn't listen and give her the support she craved. Her husband Jack said he didn't understand what she was complaining about since he always listened and tried to help. Once he understood that Iris only wanted a listener who said, "I understand why you're so upset. Do you want me to help you find a solution?"

When women want to suggest an activity, they often state it by, "Would you like to _____?" For her, that question is the start of a negotiation. But a man will often interpret the question as a literal question about his desires. He will answer yes or no, depending upon his preferences. If his answer is "no," he will just say it. If a woman later tells him that she is annoyed that her preferences were not considered, he will be upset that she is "playing games." When a man wants to do something, he will often **state** what it is that he wants. "Let's do _____!"

As women ask questions at work, oftentimes the question is interpreted as a lack of confidence or weakness. This can interfere with her having her directions followed by a man or not receiving credit for a lot of the work that she does. Other things that some women do that show weakness is the use of certain words. "Hope," "try," and "may" are examples. "I hope I can do this." "I'll try to do this." "I may be able to do this." Instead, women should use the present tense and say, "I can do this."

It is not that women or men should change their style. Rather they just need to understand the other ender's communication styles and then state what they want.

Chapter 20

For Single Moms Who Wish to Date and Have a Relationship

Because I am a social person, I wanted a social life. I also wanted to date. I got divorced when Greg was 2 years old and didn't remarry until he was 17. I learned a lot about dating in that long period when I was single. Since there are many single working mothers, I have included my thoughts about dating in this chapter. I have also included some thoughts on social support. Because time is such a limited quantity, I have talked about enjoying good relationships.

Because the divorce rate is so high, there are many women in their 30s and 40s who are single. When a man and a woman divorce, either the woman has the child most of the time or sometimes there's joint custody. I find that after so many years of marriage, people are often afraid of starting to date again. This is especially true when children are involved.

One very big issue is that of sex. Often men don't want to date a woman with children still living at home. Then there is the question of when do you go to bed with a man. What will the children think? What if a relationship lasts a few months with the man staying overnight. Then the relationship ends. Should she try for a new relationship? Will teenage children think she's promiscuous? Will younger children feel abandoned?

How will you handle sex? How do you feel about having a man stay overnight in your place while the children are in the home? Should he go home after sex and before the children wake up? How much should she let her children know? Do you feel that the only time you can have sex is when your ex has the children? Or do you feel that you will only have sex after you know that there is a solid relationship? A man that you are dating may have completely different ideas about sex. How will you resolve the differences?

Some of the fears might be....

What if the children get attached to someone and then the relationship ends?

What if the children think I am a sexual person?

What if I am taking time away from the children if I date?

What if I get involved with the wrong person?

If it happens, it happens. I don't want to look like I'm desperate.

If you are seeing a man with some regularity, or perhaps living together or even married, how will you handle discipline problems with the children if your styles are different? Does she alone handle the discipline, or is the man to take part? What if they have disagreements about how the children should be handled?

Then some women think that they will just wait and see and if a relationship is meant to be, then a man will appear. Secretly she may be longing for a man, but feels she doesn't have the time to search. If someone wants to sit around and wait, then I think of the Sleeping Beauty myth. When you're in school, it's easy to meet people. But once you're a little older and working, it's more challenging. If you want a relationship, you need to find it. I've included some exercises to help you get ready to find it and then how to narrow down your seeking.

EXERCISE:

If you are somewhat fearful but wanting to date, there is a visualization exercise you can do. The important part about this exercise is the way that you use your sensory abilities.

1. Close your eyes. Remember a time when you were successful in talking to someone or dating. Make that image bright and close and in vivid color. Add sounds and music that match. Turn images into a movie and step into it. Notice your emotional reaction.

2. Next make the picture into a still photo, step out of it, make the image small, black and white and far away. Take out the sounds. Notice your reaction.

3. Reverse the process to go back to the first image: Bright, close, vivid color, stepping into it, a movie with sound.

4. Open your eyes.

5. Close your eyes again. Now remember a time when you were not successful. Make the image bright, close in vivid color, with you in it. Notice your reaction.

6. Make the unsuccessful image small, black and white, remove self in picture and push it farther and farther away. Put in funny music, such as "Happy Birthday," or the quacking of a duck. Notice your reaction.

This is a very effective tool for changing your perception of an event. You will be surprised at how long lasting the effect is. This is a very good exercise to teach your children. It's a nice way to show them how to make memories happier and how to let go of some sad incidents.

See every problem as an opportunity to grow and learn.

EXERCISE:

If you want to have a good relationship, you might ask yourself the following question: Do you have time for a relationship?

With a friend or in front of a mirror say the following sentences out loud noticing any internal reactions that you get from any of these statements. If there is any difficulty in saying any of the statements, notice where/how it manifests in your body.

"Having a good relationship is desirable and worth it."

"It is possible to have a good relationship."

"What I need to do to achieve my goal of having a good relationship is appropriate and fits in with my life."

"I have the capabilities necessary to have a good relationship."

"I deserve and am responsible to have a good relationship."

Dating

The first few dates should be opportunities to talk a lot and get to know each other. Skip movies, entertainment, etc. because when you are spending time with him, you are not getting to know each other. Take turns planning interesting different dates where you get to converse. Instead of discussing sports, current events or the lives of famous people, get him to talk about himself in depth. Remember that your time is extremely valuable. You need to know as quickly as possible whether this man will be a suitable mate. If the answer is negative, then you need to say goodbye quickly. This is different from dating at first when the object was to have fun.

Men and women need to know that there are many differences between them. Women use conversation to feel closer and more intimate. Men feel more connection by doing things together. They use conversation to try and fix problems.

The Interview Process

Your scarcest resource is time. You need to use it wisely. **As soon as you realize that any man is not a potential partner, you must eliminate him.** Your strategy needs to be to let men tell you about themselves. Women need to remember that men love to talk about themselves. You may discover that men don't like to ask questions. You may just need to talk about yourself. Too many men have said that they have met women who seemed to have all the interests that they had until they got married and found out that the woman didn't love fishing after all.

There are 8 basic interviewing rules.

1. Direct the conversation to key topic areas: Attitudes, values, experiences, sensitive issues.
2. Let him talk.
3. Show interest and remember what he says. Use body language to show interest.
4. Do not censor his comments.
5. Do not criticize or ridicule him during the interview. Avoid expressing your own ideas until you are sure that you want to spend time with him. This is because your scarcest resource is time. Make sure that you are learning about his real values and he is not giving answers that he thinks will please you.
6. Listen to him talk about his values and interpersonal relationships. Carefully gather information about his behavior with others, because he/she is likely to behave the same way with you.
7. Ask questions that begin with "Why?"
8. What have their past relationships been like? Why did they end?

Weave these last questions in so they don't feel like they're a witness in an inquisition.

The Biggest Mistakes We Make in the Beginning of a Relationship

We don't ask enough questions. This may not seem romantic, but it's the only intelligent way to really get to know someone. Men especially may have a difficult time because culturally they are less in the habit of asking questions.

We ignore warning signs of potential problems, such as:

If he avoids discussing the past, it could be because he is hiding something serious. Are there financial or legal problems?

If he won't reveal details of family background, it may be because he has difficulty in being intimate. He may not share important feelings with you later.

If he is still in frequent contact with one or more exes, he may not be able to make a commitment to you. He may go back and forth with his feelings.

Notice his use of alcohol or drugs. If he uses a lot and gets tipsy or high often, it could be that he is an alcoholic or addicted to drugs.

If he is angry at past lovers and blames the breakups completely on them, then watch out. He hasn't learned from past mistakes. There may be one mistake that is mainly the fault of the other. But when this happens more than once, then you need to know that it will happen with you.

If he has credit problems or a larger debt than he can handle, it may mean that you'll be taking out your checkbook to help him out. Even if the amount seems trivial at first, it can escalate and become a serious problem later.

Some people want to be in charge of every aspect of the relationship. He may turn out to be a control freak and not willing to be a team player with you unless he is the leader.

Some people lose themselves too early in the relationship. I have had both men and women say to me that they operate fine, grow and do a lot of great things for themselves and with their friends—until they get involved in a relationship. Then they seem to lose themselves and lose their direction. She may decide to "keep the peace" by agreeing to his beliefs. She'll "forget" to spend time with her friends. She won't go places that she usually enjoys because, "He may not enjoy that." Then when the relationship ends, they wonder why they don't have friends. Or they'll wonder how they made such a mistake.

Although men and women are today going a little bit slower before engaging in sex, **many individuals still go to bed very early in a relationship**. Or immediately upon meeting someone they wonder if they could enjoy going to bed with that person. Physical attraction over rides the uniqueness of many individuals. Or perhaps the physical attraction to an individual is so strong that many warning signs about her are ignored.

"He has money and can take me nice places." Or he has a prestigious car. **She may just look at the outer wealth and ignore the true person.** We put commitment before compatibility. Becoming seriously involved before giving much thought to whether this person was right for you.

STOP WASTING TIME ON THE WRONG MAN!!!

Much time is wasted because many people believe that they can't ask intimate questions from their dates. Couples often date for months before they realize important personality traits in their partner. Before you get deeply emotionally involved with a potential partner you need to be aware of compatibility issues. Within the first few dates it is imperative to understand their values and what their interpersonal relationships are like. When there's a disagreement, how does he/she handle that?

Six qualities to look for in a mate.

1. Commitment to personal growth.
2. Emotional openness.
3. Integrity.
4. Maturity and responsibility.
5. High self-esteem.
6. Positive attitude toward life

EXERCISE:

A very good idea would be to look at the section on timelines in Chapter 3 and draw a timeline for your relationship. (I suggest that you use the "V" illustration so that you can learn from the past and make the adjustments in the future.) Look at your past dealings with him. When you've disagreed how have the differences been worked out? Beware if there are no differences. You need more time to evaluate this relationship. If you are not involved in a relationship right now, you can visualize your future mate as you would like him to turn out.

Walk into the future at the point where you sense that you have exactly what you want in a mate. **Fully experience** what it would be like to have this relationship now. Share with a partner or just note yourself all the situations: work, home, activities, sex life, friends, family, children, pets.

If there is anything that is not quite right about this relationship in any situation, allow a fog to roll in, blanketing that scene and let your unconscious mind fill in any missing element. Using your hands make a physical model of the person you want. Feel everything from the hair on the head to their feet.

Fully experience this right relationship.

Step off the timeline and face the present. What skills do you need to learn to reach this future? Be very specific using skills that have been mentioned in the preceding pages that you need to master (i.e., "I need to learn to be able to ask questions about his past relationships.").

Step onto the timeline in the present and look back at the past over previous relationships and notice if there are any past ties holding you back (i.e., lack of forgiveness for someone who has wronged you, parents not loving you enough, etc.). Notice if these are just tiny blips or huge emotional areas that need to be addressed. Take notes.

EXERCISE:

Here are some limiting unconscious beliefs that others have had about a great relationship. **If you have any of these beliefs, you need to release them by tapping.**

> "I've had a prior bad relationship, and I can't forgive that person."
>
> "I fear that I'll be rejected."
>
> "I can't stand the 'meat market.'"
>
> "I won't ask for what I really want."

"I continue to get into the same patterns of relationships."

"I stay with partners who don't want a relationship."

"I continually get into abusive (mental or physical) relationships."

"I believe that something bad will happen if I get into a good relationship."

"I'm not worthy of (or I don't deserve) a good relationship. This is the best I can do."

"I have the "Sleeping Beauty" myth. If I just wait, the right person will appear. No need to take any action."

"How do I know what he will be like several months from now?"

"I shouldn't judge too quickly what he is like. That's not fair."

"I know he is not the person I want, but I still want to date him."

"I love him and I know that he will change when he gets married."

"He always seems so exciting the first few months and then I lose interest."

Chapter 21

Just Say "No!"

Over the years, I have met many individuals who are unable to say "No!" They oftentimes find themselves overwhelmed both at work and their personal life because they agree to too many things they don't want to do. Mothers may get into the trap of becoming officers in the PTA or baking cookies when they'd rather read a book or watch a television program. Or they take office work home and, instead of spending quality time with their children, they are completing a work project. Or they stay late at the office.

When I ask them, why they don't say no, they have different answers:

"I don't want to hurt someone's feelings."

"I don't want to be fired."

"They really need someone, and no one else will do it."

"People won't like me."

"I'll miss an opportunity."

"He insisted on having sex (or having it his way)."

It boils down to the fact that the inability to say no is one of the most effective ways to self-sabotage yourself. If you are pleasing everyone else, when do you have the time or energy to do what you need to do for yourself?

What is the root cause of the inability to say no? It is the decisions we made as a child because of our upbringing. If our parents told us that we could never say no to them, because they were the parents, then afterwards we believe that and act accordingly. Then we pass this inability along to our children.

It is a notorious fact of life that children at the age of 2 are in their "No" stage. Of course, they can't make complete decisions for themselves at that age. However, they do not need to be reprimanded for that.

Sometimes the "No" can be honored. Or a parent can give them a choice of two actions:

"Do you want to go to bed now or in five minutes?"

"Do you want to brush your teeth first or take a bath first?"

"Do you want to wear the red or the blue dress?"

"Do you want to eat the peas before or after the chicken?"

With questions like this, a no cannot be said. The child is entertaining other thoughts.

Either way the child is learning how to make choices and learning that his choices count. This is very powerful training for a child.

EXERCISE:

But suppose as an adult you cannot say no. What can you do? This is where tapping can be extremely effective. First, you want to look at a current incident and give a number to the fear that you have about saying no. Give a number and a description of the physical sensations that you are experiencing.

Let's start there with the tapping. This is a generalized script. After doing this, it is best to remember the earliest time you felt those physical sensations when you said, "No!"

Karate Chop: (Set-up statement.) "Even though I'm afraid of saying no, I deeply and completely love and accept myself."

OR

"Even though I'm afraid people won't like me if I say no, I deeply and completely love and accept myself."

OR

"Even though I'm afraid that I'll hurt people's feelings if I say no, I deeply and completely love and accept myself."

Top of Head. "I'm so afraid that they won't like me."

Eyebrow: "I could hurt their feelings by saying no."

Side of Eye: "I don't dare say no."

Under Eye: "I'm just not good at saying no."

Under Nose: "I'll just always be a good girl."

Chin: "They really need me so I can't disappoint them."

Collarbone: "I don't dare say no."

Under Arm: "I'll just never learn to say no."

When you've reduced the number to less than 3, you might start tapping on a more positive statement.

Karate Chop: "Even though I'm not good at saying no yet, I deeply love and accept myself."

OR

"Even though I'm still afraid of saying no, I'm willing to start learning to say no."

OR

"Even though I always say yes when people ask me to do things, I'm willing to learn how to say no because I deeply and completely love and accept myself."

Top of Head: "I'm getting better at saying no."

Side of Eye: "I feel proud of myself whenever I say no."

Under Eye: "Although it's still hard to say no, I'm learning."

Under Nose: "It can actually feel good to say no."

Chin: "It's getting easier to say no."

Collarbone: "I don't have to say yes."

Under Arm: "It feels good to say no."

What are your intensity numbers now?

Now go back to a childhood memory where the physical sensations in the body or the emotions are the same and start tapping on that incident.

Now look at your life today. Are there situations where you want to say yes? Are there other situations where you want to say no? This is really about the choices that you make for your life.

For example, if at work you are asked to do a new project while you are still working on an old project, you might tell your boss something such as, "I'll be glad to do this next project. However, I am still working on the old one. How do you wish me to prioritize my time and these projects?"

As you're learning to say no, you don't want to get into an argument or discussion with that person. Don't give a long explanation. Just say something short such as, "I would like to help you out with this, but right now I am too busy." **Then keep silent.**

There might be times when there are some reasons to say yes and some reasons to say no. You might find yourself ambivalent about which answer you should give. Give yourself at least a day to make a decision. Then you can divide a sheet of paper in half with "Yes" on top of one side and "No" on top of the other. List all the yes reasons and all of the no reasons in the appropriate column. **Which side makes you honor your own goals and dreams?** That needs to be your decision.

Chapter 22

Take Care of You

How much do you care for yourself? So many clients that I see put out so much energy taking care of others—and forget to take care of themselves. Do you take time out to experience caring for yourself? Women especially tend to be caregivers. They often find it impossible to ask others for support or help. Even when their children are adults, women find it difficult to say, "I need some help."

I see women in their 40s or 50s saying, "For the first time, I'm going to take care of myself."

When children are young, and still need babysitters, the mother can tell her spouse that she is going out at least one evening a week to enjoy herself. She might have dinner with a friend or go to the movies or a museum. It's just important to carve out some regular time for herself. Just as important is a "date night" with the spouse at least once a week. Lucky are those women who have relatives who are willing to babysit. But if you don't have willing relatives nearby and child care is so expensive, find another couple with whom to trade babysitting duties.

After a divorce or separation from a loved one, some people feel very lonely. Getting a pet (especially a dog) has helped many people experience the feeling of being loved. I was walking my dogs one morning in San Diego when I slipped and fell—no fault of the dogs. Apparently one neighbor had watered his lawn too much and water on the pavement had frozen. I was not expecting ice in sunny San Diego! A neighbor saw me, drove me and my dogs home, and called Bob. The two of them helped me into his van. My dog, Zoe, knew something was wrong. She jumped on my lap, although she had never been on my lap before. I kissed her and Bob had to get her out of the van and put her inside of our house. She was protecting me and loving me to the best of her ability.

Friends are also important. Perhaps you have another human being who cares about you deeply.

Personal relationships are one of the most crucial elements of happiness and longevity. If you have close relationships, make sure to nurture them. If not, then take the time to find and nurture them.

EXERCISE:

Sit down, close your eyes, and let yourself take in the feeling of being cared about. (This could be in the past or present.) Experience that feeling in all parts of your body. After you have let yourself soak in the caring of others, change the focus to experience the feeling of you caring about you. Feel it in all parts of your body.

Now act "as if" you really do care about yourself. What does that mean? What can you do to expand on that feeling? What do you really enjoy doing for yourself? Do you take time out to savor the moment? This savoring is a very important element of happiness. This can often be done without spending any money.

Some people might want to take a hot bath, having their favorite music in the background, a scented candle lit by their side, and some herbal tea to drink. Or perhaps if you have a Jacuzzi, you could just sit in the tub and enjoy looking at a flower that you have in your yard. In San Diego, you could go to the ocean and just watch the waves come in. Take time out from work to read a good book.

I often ask clients to list three things that they could do that would make them feel extra special. Sometimes they are surprised when I tell them to do one of those things. You might also try it.

If you have the money, you might go to a fancy restaurant and enjoy a delicious dinner. Or you might buy a new outfit. Perhaps see a good play. Get a massage. Caring for yourself is extremely important for happiness. Do something extra special for yourself.

Do it! You can be pleasantly surprised at how much this can lift your morale! Get a babysitter. Rope in your spouse, a mother-in-law, or a friend to babysit for a night.

Many women, when they retire from a job that is stressful, decide that they would like to embark on another career. This second (or third) career can be following a passion that they've always had. They may need to go to school and get a degree. Or perhaps they want to paint, or start an online business.

Although the "empty nest" syndrome may be hard to get over, many people enjoy the opportunity to try something new. Others become babysitting grandparents—enjoying the children during the day, but glad to hand over responsibilities by dinnertime.

Chapter 23

Always Take In the Good

At the end of the day what do you think about? The good or the bad? Do you bawl yourself out for not doing that one thing on your to-do list, or do you congratulate yourself for accomplishing two of the things on that list? Are you upset about the snub you got at the store, or the driver that cut you off on the road? Or are you thinking of the greeting your hound gave you when you came home?

Too many of us concentrate on the negative happenings in our lives, instead of the happier ones. This is not an accident. Scientists believe that the brain has a built in *negativity* bias. Perhaps because in olden days we had to spend more time dodging stones, wild animals, and our enemies. Our lives were safer when we were prepared for dangerous incidents. Our memory of the happenings, feelings, and beliefs are increasingly negative.

But as you start thinking of the day, you might realize that you had more positive and/or neutral experiences than negative ones. Don't let the negative experiences take charge of your brain! Tilt your memories towards the happy experiences.

There is a set point of sadness and happiness that we all have. If I lose my job or miss out on an important contract, or don't get a pay raise, I might feel sadness for a certain amount of time. Then I got back to where I was before these sad incidents. If we think of this level as between a 1 and a 10, then we go back to that number. If I am generally happy about a level 6, and I fall in love or get a big promotion at work, my level might rise to an 8 or 9. Within a year I will be back at level 6. There is a way around this happiness set point. I can do some exercises to raise my happiness set point.

EXERCISE:

There is an exercise for doing this that I share with my audiences when I give public presentations. **In the evening, think of three positive experiences**

that you have had that day. Write them down in a journal. Then think of why you enjoyed them. I might say that I enjoyed my morning 3-mile walk with my dog. As I think of why I enjoyed that, I write down that I love to walk, and I love spending time with my dog. I then spend a couple of moments savoring and really enjoying that memory. Let it sink deep within your body. If you were to do this every night for six weeks, you would be guaranteed to permanently raise your happiness set point.

EXERCISE:

There is another very important exercise that I suggest families do. As you are seated around the dinner table (*and yes, I strongly encourage sitting down together away from the television at least three or four nights of the week*) **each person says three things they appreciate about each person sitting there.** There may be some repetition. But this is a very important way to build self-esteem among the family members. Every parent wants their child to be happy and this is a great step to take towards that goal.

Each person could also talk about their current undertakings. Others could ask him/her if they need any assistance.

Just be aware of any objections or reluctance that you might have to feeling positive or happy. Is it selfish or shameful to feel happy? These feelings will have to be worked through another day.

Yes, there might be the knowledge of some tough experiences you've had during the day. However, you will be more prepared to handle those challenges when you are happier.

Chapter 24

Appreciate the Special Woman You Are

When is the last time you paid attention to the simple beauty in your life?

Do you pay attention to the good things that other people do for you?

Do you grumble about the problems at work, or are you happy to have a career?

Do you complain to your spouse about his shortcomings or do you focus on the fact that you have a loving partner?

A lot of happiness is based on your perception of your life.

It is true that bad things happen to people. An experiment showed that an equal number of bad things and good things happen to most people. The big difference is in what you pay attention to. In other words, is the glass half empty or half full?

There are many ways to train your mind to appreciate your life more. Spend a few minutes a day and make an effort to think of positive things. Write about something positive that happened to you in the last few days.

One of the most important exercises to increase the happiness set point of people is to write a gratitude journal. Every night write down three things you are grateful for today.

I know that when I think of things that make me grateful, I think of my partner, Bob, the wonderful house I live in, and the fact that I live in San Diego with the best weather in the country. And, of course, I add a fourth thing to be grateful for: My two dogs.

This kind of gratitude journal should become a habit. If you do it for six weeks, you will notice a definite change in your happiness.

It's extremely difficult for a child who is in a dysfunctional unhappy home to be happy. If you are happy, you are giving a great gift to your child.

People Appreciation at Work

Our brains operate better when we are feeling happy.

When we are happier, we connect better with other people. It's even said that we might live a longer, happier life.

We perform better and think more creatively when we have very little stress. Happiness is also very important. At work this is particularly important. You want to prime your thinking to a positive pattern, as well as the thinking of subordinates, bosses, and your peer group. Emotions are contagious. Think of how people in a room were mostly in a good mood and then someone walked in with a scowl and a heavy feeling. What did that do to that gathering?

Before you think of a task to be done, or a person to talk to, take a moment and reflect on a time when you were feeling happy and creative. What made you feel this way? Was it people saying a certain thing, thinking of a fun time with your child or dog, accomplishing a special task, or something else? How can you duplicate this feeling?

EXERCISE: *Creating Positive Feelings*

One way that I have taught some students to **duplicate these positive feelings** is to make yourself comfortable somewhere where you are free from distractions. Close your eyes. Recall a time in the past when you were feeling happy and creative.

When you can feel the happiness, take the thumb and middle finger of your non-dominant hand and bring them together. Pay attention to the point where they touch and the actual pressure that is used. As you recall a time in the past when you were feeling happy, creative and a winner, remember what place you were in. Recall what you saw, heard, and felt. You may also be able to recall any smells.

When you feel these feelings of happiness and creativity, and when these feelings are strong, touch your thumb and middle finger of your non-dominant hand as before. Hold the thumb and finger together, then double the feelings. Then quadruple these feelings and hold your thumb and finger together with the same pressure as long as the feelings are strong.

When the feelings start subsiding, let go of the touch and open your eyes.

Do this several times, closing the eyes as you recall the good feelings until you can create the good feelings quickly and easily.

Next, practice this with keeping your eyes open until you can feel those good feelings quickly and easily.

Eventually, you should be able to create good feelings by touching your thumb to your finger and keeping your eyes open in this manner wherever you are. Practice duplicating that feeling until you can do it easily and rapidly. Then while you're feeling this way, give instructions to your subordinate, talk to your boss or co-workers about a project, or do what you don't want to do.

This exercise has been especially helpful to people when they have been in stressful situations. Clients have used it before an important test, doing a job interview, or making a sale. They can change their feelings by touching their thumb and middle finger and nobody knows what they are doing. (This touching is an NLP concept called *anchoring*.)

Notice the Difference in Yourself and Others When You Communicate From a Happy Mood

Now that you appreciate the good things in your life, you might wonder about getting appreciation from your family or coworkers. You give them compliments and tell them how much you appreciate their contribution to whatever you are doing. It's important to realize that people feel appreciated in different ways. Some people want to be told that what they are doing is great. Some people want a present. (And they might be particular about the kind of present they want.) Others want a touch.

The way that you feel appreciated is not the same as everyone else's. You need to communicate with others—tell them what makes you feel appreciated—and then ask what makes them feel appreciated. Give them appreciation in the way that they can take it in.

Some people cannot hear compliments, or they brush them off. Are you one of these people? You need to learn to hear compliments and instead of saying something like, "Well, anybody could (or would) do that." Just say, "thank you" and be silent. This inability to hear compliments often comes from parents who don't want to spoil the child and make him stuck up.

EXERCISE:

There is a very good exercise for couples or families at the dinner table. (Yes, families should eat together, without the television on.) Everyone at the table gives three compliments to every other person at the table. Within a month there will be a big difference in the family dynamics.

When I coach couples on their communication, one of the first skills that I teach them is how to appreciate each other. People get so busy and they take their spouse or children for granted. It has brought tears to the eyes of my clients.

Here is one last hint for a happy family. Even though you need to work and take care of the house, it is extremely important that each child gets a little bit of private time with you to talk to you, share his feelings, and the events of the day. This is important even if you only have 15 minutes for each child.

PART VI

CELEBRATE YOUR SUCCESSES & CLAIM YOUR POWER!

Chapter 25

Learn Flexibility from Great Theatre

Several years ago I returned from a two-week vacation in Ashland, Oregon—one of my favorite vacation spots. Ashland is a small town in southern Oregon that has several attractions. First and foremost are the wonderful theatre productions that they have. Second is the Bear Creek 26-mile bike and pedestrian trail. Ashland is a wonderful place to let go of all concerns and just enjoy life.

As the flier for the Oregon Shakespeare Festival states, "Women traversing their heroic, liberating and sometimes tragic paths, figure prominently in the plays of this season. Blanche Dubois in *A Streetcar Named Desire*, Eliza Doolittle in *My Fair Lady* and Kate in *The Taming of the Shrew*—all embark on life changing journeys of discovery expressed through the fiery, passionate poetry of their brilliant creators." These were three of the eleven repertory productions of that season.

I've seen all three of those plays at least once or twice before. Nevertheless, I was not bored for one minute of these productions; all three kept me enthralled every minute. Blanche is vulnerable and lives in a fantasy world. She cannot grow, **she cannot let go of the past**, and yet in the end she gains a dignity in her life. Eliza and Kate learn to take control of their lives and adjust intelligently to drastically changed circumstances.

Great theatre reminds us of our own lives, our struggles and our opportunities. Do we take charge of our own lives? Do we decide what we want in life--and then take the necessary action? Do we know how to be flexible in our reactions while still holding on to the dream?

One of the important elements of well-being is to be able to let go of the problems and traumas of the past. Counseling can help if you are stuck in the problems and traumas of the past, and they are getting in the way of your life in the present. A well-adjusted person lives in the present and plans the future. She has learned from th**e past. She is flexible and can adjust to changing circumstances. Most of all she feels in control of her life--present and future.**

All three plays held me spellbound. The music was great in *My Fair Lady*. Yes, I am passionate about good theatre. And passion, too, is an important element of happiness.

Chapter 26

Imagine What Your Life Would Be Like
if You Were Happy!

Just be aware of any objections or reluctance that you might have to feeling positive or happy. Is it selfish or shameful to feel happy? These feelings will have to be worked through another day. I asked one of my clients to tap on the statement that she had the right to be happy. She did tap and then started crying. This was a new revelation for her and although she may have said the words many times, this time those words rang in her core being. She no longer needed the stress of holding on to all the limiting beliefs that her purpose in life was to take care of others and ignore her own desires.

Yes, there might be the knowledge of some tough experiences you've had during the day. However, you will be more prepared to handle those challenges when you are happier.

This does not mean you put a rosy glow and say your life is wonderful when you have some deep issues. If you hide the issues from yourself, you won't be truly happy. That is why in tapping **you always begin with the problem**.

Rose was raising her grandson because her daughter was a drug addict. Rose always talked about how great her grandson was, and what a pleasure it was to raise him. Several years later he finally graduated from high school. She finally talked about all the difficulties she had raising him because he had so many problems. I now thought that I don't really trust Rose. She was looking through her rose-colored glasses when she described raising her grandson. Or if she admitted to herself what was really going on, she didn't share it with friends.

One of the things that I have noticed about many clients is that they very seldom seem to give themselves credit for their accomplishments. Or if they do mention an accomplishment, they will state, "But then I didn't do XXXXXXX!" They don't give themselves an opportunity to really appreciate the fact that they are improving. Many times I have had to stop a client and ask for more details on their successes. I see them relax their muscles and oftentimes they start smiling. Then they are ready to tackle the challenges in their life with a greater feeling of power.

Women in general have more difficult time than men do in bragging out their accomplishments and abilities. This holds them back in their career. If you are too bashful about bragging, then practice. You can also brag about your child. I remember when both my cousin and I were about 5 years old, my uncle put his daughter on his shoulder, marched her around the house declaring, "You are my wonderful princess! You are beautiful! You are great!" I remember feeling jealous and wishing my father would do that. My cousin grew up feeling and acting like a deserving princess, even though as an adult she was helping people. Children need to be praised for who they are and not just for what they accomplish. They need to be told that they are a joy to be with. They need to be told that you are glad to have them in your life.

What many people don't realize is that if you keep thinking about the things that you should have done but didn't—or you think of things you shouldn't have done, but did—you are setting yourself up for unhappiness. You become less satisfied with your life.

It's important that you are aware of little ways that you move forward each day. You've made five telephone calls that you needed to make. It doesn't matter if there are fifteen on the list. Congratulate yourself for five and know that tomorrow you can continue with the calling. Then consider a longer timeframe: What have you accomplished over the past twelve months? What have you grown, built, learned? What problems have you solved?

EXERCISE:

As you practice noticing your little accomplishments each day, you feel better and better about yourself. This also gives you the impetus to make bigger strides with your goals. The better we feel about ourselves, the more we can accomplish with our long term goals.

Imagine yourself in the future achieving most of the things you want in life. You are making good decisions and enjoying the life you want for yourself.

Just write in a stream of consciousness and notice a burst of inspiration that you'll probably feel.

This activity is so powerful for many reasons:

   It sets up goals for immediate work,

   It identifies deeply held values

   It presents an agenda for personal growth

You may want to think of what your ideal self might be like. Your ideal self needs to be a person that is closely aligned with your desires and goals.

Most people will feel motivated to work on themselves after this exercise. However, if you are someone who feels dejected because you are so far from being this ideal self, then you may need to write down all your accomplishments.

Another reason that this exercise is good, is because a lot of growth can be fostered by utilizing pleasant emotions.

Enjoy this exercise of discovering and inventing your ideal self.

Choices

We all have 24 hours a day. How do we choose to spend it? One of the most important choices that we make is how we spend our time. Some people work full time and the go home to take care of children and dinner. Some work full or part time at a paying job and want to start a second career with their hobby. Some people talk a lot about their new career, but spend hours playing video games or watching TV. Some people make a huge time commitment to starting a career.

What do we really want and what do we need to do to get it? Are we willing to do what it takes for success (however we define it)? Do we have the will to make this a top priority in our lives? Will we need further formal education? Do we need the cooperation of some people? Do we just need to spend the required time?

People may say they are making a choice, but then barriers get in the way. There are domestic problems, problems with low energy, friends suggesting an outing, a good TV program etc. Some people watch television for three or four hours a day. Others might play video games for hours. Obviously, they are making a choice. I had one client who told me she had great career hopes, but played video games for several hours a day, so she didn't have the energy to accomplish what she said she wanted to do.

One woman I know wanted to start a business and thought she would start with one afternoon a week. Another woman had a business plan all written out, but was too tired to do the planned work each night. Another woman wanted to start a business, but she was working full time and then spent several hours a night playing video games.

How do you get around these barriers? Where do you find the necessary time and energy to accomplish your goal?

Start with being honest with yourself. Do you really want to do this? What are the pros and cons of this idea? Can you come up with a workable realistic plan? There needs to be a passion to accomplish this goal.

Friendships

Your choices and attitudes about friendship not only have a big impact on your life and happiness, but also can tell you a lot about yourself.

Often, men and women approach friendship differently. It has been said that women have other women for their best friend, and men have their wife as a best friend. The woman who says her husband is her best friend is quite lucky indeed. Men's friendships are usually based on sharing activities, while women's friendships tend to be based on sharing intimacies about their lives. Regardless of gender, most people regard friendship as essential to their lives. Scientists are beginning to speculate that close relationships help fend off dementia in elderly people.

What is friendship? I think of a friend as someone I care about and who cares about me. We can be honest with each other about our real feelings on any area of our life. She is supportive when I have a problem, but is joyful when I triumph. When she says she will do something, I know that I can depend on her to keep her word.

As you grow as an individual, you may find that some of your friends grow with you.

Others may be lost. This is a scary subject for some people. but it is important to remember that as some friendships are lost, other will be found, and those that remain are likely to be deeper and of greater value.

EXERCISE: Who are Your Friends?

Are these people that you are proud to be with or are they just people who happen to be convenient?

Is this an equal relationship or do one of you do most of the sharing of your life?

At the end of the evening or activity that you share, do you feel energized or drained?

Do you trust these people to honor your needs and wants?

Self-Care

Do you work hard at the office and then come home and feel the house has to be perfectly clean? Is there always more to do? Perhaps you're not getting enough sleep? Are you treating yourself like a slave?

As a working mom, the idea of self-care can seem absolutely ridiculous and outrageous. "I don't have the time or energy to even think of self-care! Right now everything seems so hard and heavy."

However, if you are always drained, you cannot be a good mother or worker. You are not living up to your potential. Besides having time out, a daily ritual can also be very important. Spend a few minutes feeling gratitude for what you have experienced that day. Give yourself a foot massage. Soak in a bubble bath for a few minutes. One of the things that I love is a massage chair. The chair gives me a 15-minute workout and sometimes I am so relaxed that I can fall asleep in the chair.

EXERCISE: Self-Care Questions.

1. What kind of renewal activities do you do?
2. If you don't do any or enough, why not?
3. How often do you do renewal activities?

What else could you do?

Renewal is not a luxury—it is a necessity!

Chapter 27

Transform Yourself with Peak Performance

As you've been reading this book, you will notice that I have paid special attention to several ideas:

- You need to know what you want
- You've got to believe that it's possible for you to have it.
- If you have limiting beliefs about what is possible for you, then you need to recognize them and transform these limiting beliefs to empowering ones.
- If you have a negative critical voice (from a limiting belief) you need the change this voice into an ally to help you get what you want.
- You need to believe that you deserve to have it.
- You need to take action to get this wish.
- Never give up. There is a learning curve of changing limiting beliefs and destructive habits into empowering actions. Go for it!

What breakthrough might you make that would change your life forever?

We all have dreams about what we want to do or accomplish. Perhaps we want to be better at a particular sport. Or perhaps we want to have a lot more money. Maybe we want to have a great relationship or a home on the beach.

How can you go about actually achieving your dream?
How do you break through your personal limits?
How do you inspire yourself to new heights of excellence?

Time to challenge your beliefs about how far you can go.

EXERCISE:

Start with one or two of your highest priorities. What will this accomplish for you? Write down three limiting beliefs you have about accomplishing this.

When working with the idea of peak performance or achieving your highest goals, it's important to realize if you have any limiting beliefs about the possibility of accomplishing this. By now, you should be getting quite skilled in recognizing and tapping on limiting beliefs. This is just as important as learning the skills that play a part of peak performance.

Visualization, Affirmations & Tapping

Many people suggest that you should visualize having already achieved your goals and enjoying it. However, it is just as important to visualize any obstacles that might come up and then tap on overcoming these obstacles.

For example, say you might want a promotion at work. You could celebrate the higher salary, more interesting assignments and more flexibility in work hours. Stop and think about what could get in the way:

Perhaps someone who has no childhood rearing responsibilities is also in the running.

> You don't know if you're capable to handling the new duties.
>
> You might feel guilty about becoming the boss of some of your peers.
>
> Mostly men are in the positions of power. Why would you be selected?
>
> Some of the other workers might resent you, if you're promoted.
>
> You'll lose your friends at work.
>
> You might have to work a lot harder.
>
> You'll make more money than your husband and that might be a blow to his ego.
>
> You don't know how to tell your boss that you're the most qualified person.

These are all tapping issues. Each one of those statements that fit could be used in the Karate Chop statement.

I've covered many issues that have affected working mothers who are striving for professional success and keeping their sanity. I would like to add one more. Keep a sense of humor. It helps to be able to laugh.

I hope that this book has given you the tools to lighten the stress in your life. This is not a book about child rearing. But I do have one more word to say about child rearing. Whatever rules you give to your child, stop and think about how this will play out in later life. If you don't let your child say "No!" to you, she may grow up not knowing how to say no to requests that she does not want to follow. If you tell your child, she must finish her plate before she can leave the dinner table, she will grow up having a weight problem, because she'll eat when she has an emotional problem and will not learn when to stop eating.

If you give a child an allowance, she is learning how to manage money. If you ask your child every night about her day, she is learning to be open and honest with you. Hopefully you are asking her how she thinks she can solve any problem that comes up, rather than telling her what to do.

If you are handling your stress, overwhelm and challenges in a calm thoughtful manner, she will learn to do the same. As you tap and show your child how to tap (**Yes, tapping is a wonderful tool for children!**), she will learn how to resolve stress in her life. Your happiness and peace of mind teaches her how to have happiness and peace of mind.

TAP ON!!!

Afterword

Next Success Steps

Now that you have read and worked a lot of the exercises in ***Professional Mom's Guide to Success & Sanity*** you are well on your way from the haggard, frazzled, stressed out mother to the calm, peaceful, and successful woman you were always meant to be.

If you find that the exercises feel too difficult or you feel too emotional when you try to work with them, it will help to work with a qualified coach or licensed counselor.

I am so happy that you've succeeded in working through much of this book. I have been so excited to see so many of my clients reach their goals.

I have recorded six "tap along" MP3 audios to help you become an expert tapper as a special bonus for you. All you need to do is to go to my website and register for these bonuses and I will e-mail them to you.

Go to http://www.sheilahenry.com/Bonus.en.html to register for your gift. Your information is private and will not be shared with anyone. As another bonus, you will also receive tips and information on stress from time to time.

The sooner you know how to manage stress, the sooner you'll feel in control. The sooner you conquer a lot of your stress, the healthier your children will be.

Best of health, wealth and joy.

Sheila

Acknowledgements

I wish to acknowledge my many teachers and coaches who have mentored and helped me grow both professionally and personally over the years.

Pamela Bruner, my lead business coach, for working patiently with me on both business strategy and mindset.

Diana M. Needham, business coach and member of Pamela Bruner's team, for giving me the inspiration (and a lot of technical help) to write this book.

Heidi Thorne, my editor, for her patience and focus on polishing this book and smoothing out all the rough edges

Gene Monterastelli, tapping coach and also a member of Pamela Bruner's team, for his wonderful expertise with not only tapping but productivity and organizational skills.

Dale Teplitz, my EFT (Emotional Freedom Techniques—commonly known as "tapping") teacher.

All the other teachers I've had over many years.

About the Author

Sheila Henry is a licensed Marriage Counselor in California. She has worked with individuals, groups, and couples for over 30 years. She has studied many forms of psychotherapy including Cognitive Therapy, Gestalt, Ericksonian hypnosis, NLP, and finally EFT (Emotional Freedom Techniques) also known as "tapping".

She has been especially impressed with the rapidity and effectiveness of EFT. Because EFT combines acupressure points with Western psychotherapy, it is capable of healing traumas, chronic pain, anxiety, depression, and other ailments. It is also effective in working with individuals trying to reach peak performance goals.

She has a Master's Degree in psychology from Lone Mountain, University of San Francisco.

Sheila has a private practice in San Diego, California, where she works with individuals and groups. She lives with her partner, Robert Cook, and two Malinois dogs. She enjoys walking, Tai Chi, Qi Gong, murder mysteries, Rotary, and visiting with friends.

She can be contacted on her website: www.SheilaHenry.com.

www.ingramcontent.com/pod-product-compliance
Lightning Source LLC
LaVergne TN
LVHW021457080426
835509LV00018B/2320